CIVIL RIGHTS
The law, the police, and you

P. Michael Bolton, B.A., LL.B.

Self-Counsel Press
(a division of)
International Self-Counsel Press Ltd.
Vancouver
Toronto   Seattle

Copyright © 1971, 1989 by International Self-Counsel Press Ltd.

All rights reserved.

No part of this book may be reproduced or transmitted in any form by any means without permission from the publisher, except by a reviewer who may quote brief passages in a review.

Printed in Canada

First edition: December, 1971
Second edition: December, 1972
Third edition: August, 1973
Fourth edition: June, 1975
Fifth edition: September, 1976
Sixth edition: October, 1978
Seventh edition: February, 1984
Eighth edition: October, 1985
Ninth edition: February, 1989

Canadian Cataloguing in Publication Data

    Bolton, P. Michael (Philip Michael), 1943 -
    Civil Rights: the law, the police, and you

    (Self-counsel legal series)
    ISBN 0-88908-854-3

    1. Civil rights — Canada — Popular works.
I. Title.   II. Series
KE4381.B64   1989   342.71'085   C89-091068-5

Cartoons by Matt McLean

Self-Counsel Press
(a division of)
International Self-Counsel Press Ltd.
1481 Charlotte Road
North Vancouver, British Columbia V7J 1H1

CONTENTS

INTRODUCTION		xix
1	**CONSTITUTIONAL RIGHTS OF CANADIANS**	**1**
a.	Fundamental freedoms	1
b.	Right to life, liberty, and security of the person	1
c.	Right to be secure against unreasonable search or seizure	2
d.	Right not to be arbitrarily detained or imprisoned	3
e.	Right of person who has been arrested or detained to be informed promptly of the reasons	4
f.	Right to retain and instruct counsel without delay and to be informed of that right	4
g.	Right of person charged with an offence to be informed without unreasonable delay of the specific offence	5
h.	Right to have a trial within a reasonable time	6
i.	Right to be presumed innocent	6
j.	Right to reasonable bail	7
k.	Right to jury trial	7
l.	Right against self-incrimination	7
m.	Right to an interpreter	8
n.	Equality rights	8
o.	Government infringement of rights	9
p.	The "notwithstanding" clause	9
q.	Restriction in the use of illegally obtained evidence	10
r.	Other remedies for violation of civil rights	10
s.	The status of our new constitutional rights	11

2 THE RIGHTS OF SUSPECTS — 12
  a. The general rules: The right to remain silent — 12
  b. The right to counsel — 13
  c. The right to a telephone call — 13
  d. Admissions and confessions — 13
  e. Oral statements to police — 14
  f. What makes a person a suspect? — 15
  g. Police at your residence, office, or workplace — 15
  h. The basic rules of search and seizure — 16
  i. Some exceptions to the general rules on search and seizure — 17
  j. Search of person — 19
  k. Can a person be arrested for investigation? — 20
  l. Be diplomatic — 21
  m. Powers of police officers — 22
  n. Police in a public place: what will arouse suspicion? — 22
  o. Reasons for stopping people in public places — 23
  p. Drivers — 25
  q. Investigation of drinking and driving cases — 25

3 THE LAW OF ARREST — 27
  a. Summary and indictable offences: what's the difference? — 27
  b. Indictable offences — 27
  c. Summary offences — 28
  d. The arrest — 28
  e. Constitutional rights at the time of arrest — 28
  f. Illegal arrests — 29
  g. Citizen's arrest — 30
  h. Charged but not arrested — 30

4	**THE CONSEQUENCES OF AN ARREST**	32
	a. The right to remain silent after an arrest	33
	b. Is silence always wise?	33

5	**BOOKED, FINGERPRINTED, AND PHOTOGRAPHED**	36
	a. Don't talk about your charge	36
	b. Your right to a bail hearing	38
	c. Your right to counsel	38
	d. Right to be informed of the specific charge against you	38
	e. How long are you kept in custody?	39
	f. Fingerprints and photographs	40

6	**FURTHER RIGHTS OF AN ACCUSED PERSON**	41
	a. Line-ups and show-ups	42
	b. Showing photographs to witnesses	43
	c. Polygraph tests	43
	d. Police demand for fingerprints and photographs where accused not charged with indictable offence	44
	e. Handwriting samples	44
	f. Samples of breath, urine, or blood	45

7	**TYPES OF PARTICIPATION IN A CRIME**	46
	a. Principals to the offence and aiding and abetting	46
	b. Joint commission of crime	47
	c. Joint possession	47
	d. Attempts	47
	e. Counselling or procuring	48
	f. Accessory after the fact	48
	g. Compounding an indictable offence	49
	h. Conspiracy	49

8 SEARCH AND SEIZURE IN THE CRIMINAL CODE: GENERAL PROVISIONS — 50
   a. Requirement for a search warrant — 50
   b. Your rights when presented with a search warrant — 50
   c. Search of motor vehicle — 52
   d. Telewarrants — 54
   e. Remedies for illegal search or seizure — 54
   f. Review of basis for issuing search warrant — 55
   g. Solicitor and client privilege — 55

9 SEARCH AND SEIZURE IN THE CRIMINAL CODE: SPECIAL PROVISIONS RELATING TO GAMBLING, BETTING, OBSCENITY, AND PROSTITUTION CASES — 57
   a. Gambling and betting — 57
   b. Search of gambling and betting houses — 58
   c. Search of gaming house without warrant — 58
   d. Arrest and questioning of found-ins — 59
   e. Search of a common bawdy house — 59
   f. Found-ins in a bawdy house — 60
   g. Obscenity cases — 60

10 SEARCH AND SEIZURE UNDER THE INCOME TAX LAWS — 62
   a. Offences under the Income Tax Act — 62
   b. General powers of auditors — 63
   c. Power of an auditor to seize documents — 63
   d. Demand letter for information — 64
   e. Search warrants under the Income Tax Act — 64
   f. Seizure of documents from a lawyer's office — 65
   g. Examination of bank documents — 65
   h. Statements made to auditors or investigators — 66

	i. The compliance rule	66
11	**THE NARCOTICS LAWS**	67
	a. Possession	68
	b. Cultivation	68
	c. Trafficking	69
	d. Possession for the purpose of trafficking	69
	e. Importing	70
12	**THE FOOD AND DRUGS ACT**	71
	a. Restricted drugs	71
	b. Penalties for possession of restricted drugs	71
	c. Trafficking in restricted drugs	71
	d. Controlled drugs	72
	e. Possession of controlled drugs not an offence	72
	f. Trafficking in controlled drugs	73
13	**THE DRUG LAWS — SEARCH AND SEIZURE**	74
	a. Search of person	75
	b. Search of vehicle	75
	c. Illegal searches	76
	d. Search of residence	76
	e. Telewarrants	77
14	**DRUG TRIALS — WHAT THE PROSECUTOR MUST PROVE**	78
	a. Why retain a lawyer?	79
	b. Incriminating evidence	79
	c. Should the accused testify?	79
	d. Involuntary possession	80
15	**DRINKING AND DRIVING LAWS**	82
	a. What are the drinking and driving offences?	82

	b.	What kind of evidence causes police to stop a vehicle?	84
	c.	Rights of the driver who is stopped and questioned	85
	d.	Do police have the right to search a suspected impaired driver?	85
	e.	Search of vehicle	86
	f.	What factors may lead police to charge a driver?	86
	g.	Physical tests	87
	h.	Statements of suspects	87
	i.	Breathalyzer tests	88
	j.	The demand for breathalyzer tests	88
	k.	Blood samples	88
	l.	Right to a lawyer	89
16	**THE LIQUOR LAWS**		92
	a.	Beer and wine produced for personal use	92
	b.	Liquor offences under federal revenue laws	93
	c.	Search and seizure under federal liquor laws	93
	d.	Offences under provincial liquor laws	94
	e.	Search and seizure under provincial liquor laws	95
17	**SEARCH AND SEIZURE UNDER THE CUSTOMS LAWS: BORDER SEARCHES**		96
	a.	Arriving at the Canadian border	97
	b.	Search of person	97
	c.	Search of baggage and vehicle	98
	d.	Search of a building or warehouse	99
	e.	Writs of assistance	99
	f.	Arrest without a warrant	100
	g.	Seizure and forfeiture of goods	100
	h.	Seizure and forfeiture of vehicle	100

	i.	Airport searches	101
18	**IMMIGRATION LAWS: TOURISTS AND VISITORS**		102
	a.	Who may not visit?	103
	b.	Visit by ministerial permit	104
	c.	What may immigration officers demand?	104
	d.	Student and work visas	105
	e.	Medical examinations	105
	f.	Groups of performers and athletes	106
	g.	Temporary visits of business representatives	106
	h.	Employment authorizations	106
	i.	Who may be deported?	107
	j.	Right of detained person to have legal counsel and interpreter	108
19	**IMMIGRATION, POLITICAL ASYLUM, AND EXTRADITION**		109
	a.	Immigrating to Canada	109
	b.	Who may not immigrate?	109
	c.	Arrest and bail	110
	d.	Political asylum and extradition	111
	e.	Canadians travelling to foreign countries	112
20	**THE WEAPONS LAWS**		114
	a.	Is there a right to possess firearms?	115
	b.	Revolvers (restricted weapons)	115
	c.	Permit to move a restricted weapon	117
	d.	Refusal or revocation of permit or certificate	117
	e.	Prohibited weapons	118
	f.	Possession of a weapon for a dangerous purpose	118
	g.	The right to self-defence	119

21	**LAW OF PUBLIC MEETINGS**	121
	a. Freedom of association and peaceful assembly	121
	b. Constitutional limits on fundamental freedoms	121
	c. A further constitutional limit: the opting out clause	122
	d. Definition of unlawful assembly	122
	e. Riots	123
	f. Disturbances	124
	g. Picketing	125
	h. Arrest at an unlawful disturbance or assembly	125
	i. Post-arrest procedures	127
22	**SEX AND THE LAW**	128
	a. Statutory rape	128
	b. Prostitution	129
	c. Abortion	131
	d. Venereal diseases	131
	e. Nudity	131
	f. Indecent act or performance	132
	g. Gross indecency	133
23	**BAIL: RELEASE BY POLICE OFFICERS**	134
	a. Appearance notice issued by attending officer	134
	b. Release after arrest	136
	c. Release by officer-in-charge	136
	d. Right to appear before a justice or judge	137
24	**HOW AND WHEN DO YOU GET BAIL?**	138
	a. Your right to a bail hearing	138
	b. Reasonable bail	138
	c. Bail Reform Act and amendments	138
	d. Cases where prosecutor must show cause	139

NOTICE TO READERS

Laws are constantly changing. Every effort is made to keep this publication as current as possible. However, neither the author nor the publisher can accept any responsibility for changes to the law or practice that occur after the printing of this publication. Please be sure that you have the most recent edition.

	e.	Non-residents	140
	f.	Bail with conditions	140
	g.	Remand for observation	140
	h.	Bail with agreement of prosecutor	140
	i.	Procedure at a bail hearing	141
	j.	Cash bail, surety, and recognizance	141
	k.	Illegal to indemnify bondsmen	142
	l.	Consequences of a failure to appear	142
	m.	Turning in the accused	143
	n.	Arrest in another province	143
25	**DENIAL OF BAIL AND OTHER DIFFICULTIES**		145
	a.	Denial of bail	145
	b.	Appeal from detention order	145
	c.	Cases where accused must show cause	145
	d.	The most serious cases	146
	e.	Right to trial within a reasonable time	147
	f.	Delay of trial in cases of detention	147
	g.	Proposed criminal code changes	148
	h.	Remands	148
	i.	Violation of bail	148
	j.	The accused in custody	149
26	**BEFORE THE TRIAL**		150
	a.	The wisdom of having a lawyer	150
	b.	Legal fees	151
	c.	Legal aid	151
	d.	The trial date	151
	e.	Right to be informed without unreasonable delay	152
	f.	Particulars	152

g.	Application for formal particulars	153
h.	Arraignment	154
i.	Right to a jury trial	154
j.	Preliminary hearings	155
k.	Proposal for pre-trial conferences	156
l.	Plea bargaining	157
m.	Stay of proceedings	158
n.	Motions to quash	159
o.	Motion for a separate trial	159

27 THE COURSE OF THE TRIAL — 161

a.	Adjournments of the trial	162
b.	Is the accused required to be present throughout the trial?	163
c.	The trial of corporations	165
d.	Trial in open court	166
e.	The presumption of innocence	167
f.	Right to remain silent	167
g.	The right to make full answer and defence	167
h.	Courtroom manners	167
i.	Mistrials and hung juries	168
j.	Appeals	169

28 THE RIGHTS OF WITNESSES — 170

a.	The right of a witness to have a lawyer	170
b.	Witness under subpoena	171
c.	Subpoena of documents	171
d.	Material witness warrant	172
e.	Attacking the subpoena	172
f.	Refusal of witness to answer questions	173
g.	Taking the oath	173

	h.	Husband or wife as witness	173
	i.	The accused as witness	175
	j.	Solicitor/client privilege	175
	k.	Self-incrimination	176
	l.	Obstruction of justice	177
29	**ROLE OF THE PRESS IN CRIMINAL PROCEEDINGS: PUBLICATION AND BROADCAST OF EVIDENCE OF PROCEEDINGS**		178
	a.	Limits on the press after arrest of the accused: Criminal contempt	179
	b.	What is the press entitled to publish?	180
	c.	Reporting of bail hearing	180
	d.	At the preliminary hearing	181
	e.	Publication or broadcast of a confession	182
	f.	Motion for change of venue	182
	g.	Motion for mistrial	183
	h.	Publication of evidence during trial	183
30	**DISCHARGES, CONVICTIONS, AND SENTENCES**	185
	a.	Absolute and conditional discharges	185
	b.	What will the judge consider on an application for discharge?	186
	c.	When you are convicted	187
	d.	Intermittent sentences	188
	e.	The abolition of capital punishment	188
31	**CRIMINAL RECORDS**	189
	a.	Consequences of a criminal record	189
	b.	Application for pardon	190
	c.	Effect of a pardon	191

	d. Is there a criminal record where a person is acquitted?	192
	e. Request to destroy fingerprints and photographs	193
32	**YOUNG OFFENDERS**	**194**
	a. What offences are dealt with in youth court?	194
	b. Policy of the law in dealing with young offenders	195
	c. Arrest of young offenders	195
	d. Fingerprinting and photographing of young offenders	196
	e. Right to counsel	196
	f. Notice to parents	197
	g. Disposition of cases	197
	h. Trials in youth court	198
	i. Transfer to ordinary court	198
	j. Protection of privacy of young persons	199
33	**ELECTRONIC SURVEILLANCE BY POLICE**	**200**
	a. What types of communications can be legally intercepted?	200
	b. Procedures to be followed for legal wiretaps	201
	c. What offences can be investigated by wiretapping?	202
	d. Conversations with undercover agents or informers	203
	e. How long does a wiretap continue?	204
	f. Does a suspect have the right to know if his or her phone has been wiretapped?	204
	g. Does a person have any right to prevent wiretaps?	205
	h. What are the penalties for illegal wiretapping?	205

	i.	What use can be made of evidence obtained through wiretaps?	205
	j.	Conversations with lawyers	206
34	**REMEDIES**	207
	a.	What can you do?	207
	b.	Civil actions for abuse of authority	208
	c.	Criminal charges for abuse of authority	210
	d.	The effect of the charter of rights and freedoms	211
	e.	Remedies available under section 24(1)	212
	f.	Remedies available under section 24(2)	214

APPENDIX

Constitution Act, 1982   217

INTRODUCTION

This edition of *Civil Rights* coincides with a new era in the evolution of the civil rights of Canadians. This new era arises primarily because our country now has a written constitution. The Constitution Act, 1982, became the law of the land on April 17, 1982. It contains the Charter of Rights and Freedoms, providing constitutional guarantees of legal rights.

The new constitutional rights are described and summarized in chapter 1. Discussion of them appears in numerous other chapters. It is expected that the Charter will ultimately have a profound effect on Canadian laws, but it is far too early to predict specifically how the courts will interpret and apply its provisions.

Before 1982, there was no constitutional protection of civil rights for Canadians. The Bill of Rights was a simple statute of Parliament that could be repealed or amended at the whim of a majority of the members of Parliament. The Bill of Rights was and remains (it has not been repealed) a rhetorical statement of civil rights; however, because it is not a constitutional document, it cannot override other federal legislation. It does not apply at all to the provinces.

The new Constitution, including the Charter of Rights and Freedoms, is "entrenched" in the sense that it cannot be repealed or amended by the legislature of any province or the federal government. Therefore, the rights and freedoms are thought to be beyond the reach of the provincial legislatures or of Parliament. The Constitution is the supreme law, and any other law that is inconsistent with it is deemed to be of "no force or effect."

However, there is a provision in Section 33 of the Constitution that permits Parliament or a province to opt out of the fundamental freedoms and legal rights in the Charter. A government can do this simply by declaring in a particular statute that it shall operate notwithstanding one of the fundamental freedoms or legal rights in the Charter. Such an opting out provision is valid for five years, but can be renewed for a further five-year period.

The equality rights provision of the Charter came into effect on April 7, 1985 under Section 15 of the Charter, which provides that "every individual is equal before and under the law and has the right to the equal protection and equal benefit of the law without discrimination and, in particular, without discrimination based on race, national or ethnic origin, color, religion, sex, age, or mental or physical disability."

Since the new Constitution came into effect, there have been constitutional challenges to many existing legal procedures. For example, writs of assistance have been successfully attacked and declared void on the basis that they violate the right under the Charter to be secure against unreasonable search or seizure.

Writs of assistance were a kind of search warrant issued to a police officer for the life of his or her career with the force. They enabled the officer to search any premises at any time on the basis of a reasonable belief that narcotics (or evidence of certain other federal offences) could be found. Ordinary search warrants require a police officer to swear on an information before a justice of the peace that evidence of a particular crime can be found at a particular place, and they are valid only for that one specific search. This judicial scrutiny was dispensed with by writs of assistance. The Supreme Court of Canada found that the writs lent themselves to potential arbitrary use and therefore declared them to be in violation of Section 8 of the Charter.

To replace the writs of assistance, the Criminal Code was amended to include a provision for the telewarrant, an authorization to search which is obtained orally from a justice of the peace over the telephone or via some other form of telecommunication.

To obtain a telewarrant, a police officer must have reasonable grounds for a search, and the circumstances must be such that it is impracticable to obtain an ordinary search warrant, for example, when a delay might lead to loss of evidence. The officer telephones a justice of the peace or a judge, explains why a telewarrant is necessary, and provides the usual details of the persons and premises to be searched, the offences for which the evidence is being sought, and grounds for the search. This call is tape recorded and a transcript made. When a search is authorized, a written version or facsimile of the oral authorization must be provided before entry or as soon as practicable thereafter to the persons whose premises are being searched.

The major change with the new Constitution is an expanded role for the courts in making laws. Historically, the Supreme Court of Canada, unlike its American counterpart, was restrained in this area. The Constitution creates a new role of lawmaking for the court in deciding constitutional issues.

Civil Rights explains the civil and constitutional rights that Canadians have in dealing with the criminal justice system. The book is intended as a starting point for understanding legal rights and obligations as well as criminal laws and procedures. It is not exhaustive; nor are any comments in the book to be taken as the final word on the law to be applied in a given situation. Experience with the law and legal procedures teaches that each situation needs to be judged on its own facts and merits.

Therefore, there is no substitute for consulting a lawyer when you have problems arising from relations with the police or a case in the courts. Familiarity with the information contained in this book will enable you to discuss your situation with more knowledge and awareness, but it is not a substitute for legal advice.

1
CONSTITUTIONAL RIGHTS OF CANADIANS

a. FUNDAMENTAL FREEDOMS

Fundamental freedoms are defined in Section 2 of the Charter of Rights and Freedoms. They include the following:

(a) Freedom of conscience and religion

(b) Freedom of thought, belief, opinion, and expression including freedom of the press and other media of communication

(c) Freedom of peaceful assembly

(d) Freedom of association

Prior to 1982, these rights were considered to be part of the common law, but they did not have constitutional protection. Freedom of peaceful assembly and freedom of association are dealt with in chapter 21, "Law of Public Meetings."

b. RIGHT TO LIFE, LIBERTY, AND SECURITY OF THE PERSON

Section 7 of the Charter provides that everyone has the right to "life, liberty, and security of the person and the right not to be deprived thereof except in accordance with the principles of fundamental justice."

At minimum, this right gives everyone whose liberty is at stake, such as in criminal proceedings, the right to be dealt with in accordance with the "principles of fundamental justice." These principles include basic fairness, such as the right to fully understand the charge against one, to have the opportunity to defend the charge, and to make full answer and defence to the allegations and other basic principles of fairness. These could include the obligation of the Crown in all criminal cases to prove the case against the subject beyond a reasonable doubt. Section 7 is similar to the due process clause in the United States Constitution, which has received very broad interpretation in the U.S. courts; it is an important source of protection against arbitrary actions by police, prosecutors, or judicial officers.

c. RIGHT TO BE SECURE AGAINST UNREASONABLE SEARCH OR SEIZURE

This is an important new right for Canadians. Already the Supreme Court of Canada has handed down a wide-reaching decision in which it sets out the standard of reasonableness for conducting a search. In its judgment, the court has held that a person authorizing a search, acting judicially, must assure him or herself on the evidence that the search warrant ought to be issued. In the absence of this proper consideration, the search warrant may be held to be invalid and any evidence thereby obtained excluded from court. The Supreme Court decided that the right to be secure against unreasonable search or seizure extends beyond mere protection of property and that the interest to be protected is the individual's reasonable expectation of privacy.

Other courts have held that in order to ensure the right to make full answer and defence, an accused person ought to have access to the information that was before the judge or justice of the peace who issued the search warrant. Problems of confidentiality of sources, the courts have held, can be dealt with by judicial editing of the names of persons who need to be protected from disclosure. In this way, a proper assessment may then be made as to whether a reasonable standard was met by the issuing justice.

There have also been a number of cases in which the courts have rejected evidence obtained by police through unreasonable searches. For example, evidence has been rejected when a police officer had a mere suspicion that a person might possess an illegal substance, since this suspicion did not amount to reasonable cause for a search. In these kinds of circumstances, if the court finds that the search is unreasonable, it can exclude the evidence on the basis that to use it would "bring the administration of justice into disrepute."

Similar protection exists for people passing through customs. Unless the customs officer has reasonable grounds for believing that a person is carrying contraband, the search is in violation of a person's right to be secure from unreasonable search or seizure. However, there is still division in Canadian courts on these issues and they have yet to be finally resolved.

d. RIGHT NOT TO BE ARBITRARILY DETAINED OR IMPRISONED

It has always been unlawful to arbitrarily detain or imprison a person. However, a person arbitrarily detained by police or other public investigators did not have a remedy except to lay charges in civil law. Evidence obtained illegally could still be used at the trial of a criminal charge against the person wrongfully detained.

The new constitutional protection of the right not to be arbitrarily detained makes a substantial change in the law. Now, when a person has been unlawfully detained and evidence has been obtained against that person because of that unlawful detention, the court has the power to exclude the evidence from the trial if its use would bring the administration of justice into disrepute.

Arbitrary detention might arise when a person has been detained, but not arrested or charged, for the purpose of further investigation. There is no law that permits arrest for investigation. An arrest must be for the purpose of charging a person, or else it is illegal.

Violation of the right against arbitrary detention might arise where store detectives or other private security personnel detain a person with the intention of having police investigate an alleged crime. If security personnel do not have the evidence to support a charge and are not making a citizen's arrest, such detention may be arbitrary and lead to the rejection of evidence in a subsequent criminal case. It could, of course, also lead to civil actions against persons responsible for the arbitrary detention.

e. RIGHT OF PERSON WHO HAS BEEN ARRESTED OR DETAINED TO BE INFORMED PROMPTLY OF THE REASONS

A police officer who makes an arrest is required by law to give the arrested person a reason for the arrest. This has always been part of the common law, and now there is a constitutional right "to be informed promptly of the reasons" for the arrest or detention.

The word "promptly" in this context mean immediately or as soon as possible. The Criminal Code requires that a person arrested and charged with a criminal offence must be brought before a justice of the peace as soon as possible or within 24 hours of the time of arrest.

Police are not expected to give details, but a general statement of the charge against the person must be given.

f. RIGHT TO RETAIN AND INSTRUCT COUNSEL WITHOUT DELAY AND TO BE INFORMED OF THAT RIGHT

This clause in Section 10 of the Charter of Rights and Freedoms marks a substantial departure from the common law and the Bill of Rights.

Police under Canadian law now have an obligation to tell the accused person that he or she has the right to retain and instruct counsel without delay. Canadians have always had the this right, but unless they knew about and insisted on it, the right had little meaning.

Under the new rules, a police officer must inform the accused of the right to have a lawyer. If the police officer fails to inform the accused, the arrest is unlawful and a violation of constitutional rights under Section 10 of the Charter.

This could lead a court to reject evidence on the basis of infringement of constitutional rights where the court takes the view that the use of such evidence would bring the administration of justice into disrepute.

In addition, courts can grant to the accused a range of other remedies, such as a stay of proceedings or dismissal of the charges, where his or her rights as guaranteed by the Constitution have been infringed or denied. These rights are in addition to the classic remedies of suing for damages for illegal arrest or malicious prosecution.

Canadians now enjoy the same constitutional rights on arrest as Americans. For years, Canadians have been subjected to American television shows in which police are required to tell an arrested person of the right to have a lawyer, only to find that such requirements did not exist in Canada. Now reality is in accord with the TV myth.

There is still no specific requirement in Canada that an accused person be warned that any statements made to a police officer may be used in evidence against him or her.

The right to counsel includes the right to have a reasonable opportunity to contact counsel, which the courts have interpreted to include access to a telephone and the right to make as many calls as are reasonably necessary. It also includes the right to speak with counsel on the telephone in private, which means without police officers being present or in a position to overhear the conversation.

The right to counsel may also include the right to have legal aid counsel, where an accused is unable to afford counsel. The United States Constitution has been interpreted as requiring the state to provide effective legal assistance for a person who cannot afford his or her own lawyer.

g. **RIGHT OF PERSON CHARGED WITH AN OFFENCE TO BE INFORMED WITHOUT UNREASONABLE DELAY OF THE SPECIFIC OFFENCE**

We have already seen that a person who is arrested has the right to be informed promptly of the reasons for the arrest. In addition, once a person has been charged with an offence, he or she has the right to be informed without an unreasonable delay of the specific charge. This would normally happen under Criminal Code requirements; however, there may occasionally be cases in which the constitutional protection is important. It is expected that the words "unreasonable delay" may mean in excess of 24 hours. Normally, a person charged with a criminal offence must be charged with the specific offence in a document known as an "information" within 24 hours.

h. RIGHT TO HAVE A TRIAL WITHIN A REASONABLE TIME

A person charged with an offence in Canada now has the right to be tried within a reasonable time. It may be a misnomer to say that this is a right to a speedy trial, and much depends on how the courts interpret "reasonable."

The Supreme Court of Canada has ruled that the right to have a trial within a reasonable time is such a fundamental right that the minimum remedy available when this right is violated is a "stay" (i.e., an end of the proceedings against the accused).

Although the Supreme Court of Canada has held that delay before being charged is not to be considered when determining whether the right to have a trial within a reasonable time has been violated, such pre-charge delay may affect an accused's right to a fair trial and his or her ability to make full answer and defence. This issue has not been finally determined.

i. RIGHT TO BE PRESUMED INNOCENT

An accused person has the right to be presumed innocent until proven guilty "according to law in a fair and public hearing by an independent and impartial tribunal." Once again, the presumption of innocence has always been part of our law, but it did not enjoy constitutional protection.

An important case decided by the Supreme Court of Canada held that the reverse onus provisions under the Narcotic Control Act and the Food and Drugs Act violated this right under the Charter. In those statutes, it was provided that a person in possession of a drug, even a small amount, was presumed to be in possession for the purpose of trafficking if the prosecutor had laid the possession for the purpose of trafficking charge.

The court held that this put the accused in the position of having to establish his or her innocence and struck down the legislation as being contrary to the presumption of innocence.

j. RIGHT TO REASONABLE BAIL

Section 11(e) of the Charter provides that a person charged with an offence has the right "not to be denied reasonable bail without just cause."

Once again, this right has always existed in Canadian law, but it did not previously have constitutional protection. There are numerous provisions in Canadian law in which the onus is on the accused to show that he or she should be released on bail. This is the case, for example, where the accused is charged with possession for the purpose of trafficking a narcotic.

Many of the "reverse onus" provisions under the bail laws are being challenged on the basis that they constitute a denial of reasonable bail without just cause. It remains to be seen how successful these challenges will be. We can expect to wait a few years before the ground rules on bail laws under the Constitution are clearly defined by the courts.

k. RIGHT TO JURY TRIAL

A person charged with an offence has the right to a jury trial where the maximum penalty for the offence is imprisonment for five years or more.

This excludes such offences as impaired driving, common assault, theft or possession of stolen property under $200, and a range of other minor criminal offences.

It also excludes all summary conviction offences, such as causing a disturbance, unlawful assembly, or possession of a drug, where the Crown elects to proceed summarily, as is usually the case in soft drug offences.

l. RIGHT AGAINST SELF-INCRIMINATION

Persons charged with an offence have the right not to be compelled to be a witness in proceedings against themselves. This means that you cannot be compelled to testify at your own trial. You and your counsel may decide that you should testify, but the Crown cannot require it. This is a constitutional entrenchment of the common law rule that the accused has the right to remain silent throughout the trial.

In addition, Section 13 of the Constitution gives a witness who testifies in any case a right not to have any incriminating evidence given used against that witness in any other proceedings, except a prosecution for perjury.

The basic protection against future use of self-incriminating statements is also available to a witness under the Canada Evidence Act. That procedure is discussed in chapter 28.

To obtain the protection of the Canada Evidence Act, a witness must object to answering the question on the ground that the answer may tend to incriminate him or her. Now, the Charter also provides that a witness who testifies has an absolute right not to have "any incriminating evidence he or she gives used to incriminate that witness in any other proceedings" except a perjury charge.

m. RIGHT TO AN INTERPRETER

Section 14 of the Charter provides that a party or a witness in a proceeding who does not understand or speak the language in which the proceeding is conducted or who is deaf has the right to have the assistance of an interpreter.

In addition, Section 19 provides that English or French may be used by any person in any court established by Parliament.

n. EQUALITY RIGHTS

While it is too early to measure the full impact of the equality rights provisions of the Charter on Canadian laws, it is already apparent that this has become an effective tool for challenging legislation. This section provides a constitutional right for every individual to be equal before and under the law and to equal protection and equal benefit of the law without discrimination. To date most of the successful challenges have been in areas of law other than criminal law.

The equality rights provisions specifically prohibit discrimination based on race, national or ethnic origin, color, religion, sex, age, and mental or physical disability. However, discrimination on other unspecified grounds is also prohibited and the specific areas of prohibited discrimination are not exhaustive.

So-called affirmative action programs, programs for the amelioration of conditions of disadvantaged individuals or groups, which in a sense are discriminatory against other groups, are an exception to the forms of prohibited discrimination. For example, a provincial law designed to encourage the employment of Native Indians in a given area of the province, with the object of bettering the conditions of those persons, could not be challenged under the anti-discrimination clause.

Many of the early challenges have been directed against governmental programs restricting access to employment, such as mandatory retirement schemes.

o. GOVERNMENT INFRINGEMENT OF RIGHTS

The government can invade the rights and freedoms guaranteed by the Charter by relying on Section 1, which provides that the rights and freedoms guaranteed in the Charter are guaranteed "subject only to such reasonable limits prescribed by law as can be demonstrably justified in a free and democratic society." This limit applies to all of the rights set out in the Charter.

There is very little guidance from the courts at the moment as to what constitutes a reasonable limit, what is meant by "prescribed by law," and to what extent can "reasonable limits" on our rights be said to be "demonstrably justified" in the "free and democratic society." The government bears the burden of justifying an infringement of rights.

p. THE "NOTWITHSTANDING" CLAUSE

Another means by which governments can limit the operation of the Charter of Rights and Freedoms is by using the "notwithstanding" clause in Section 33. This section provides that Parliament or a provincial legislature may expressly declare that legislation will operate notwithstanding a conflict with the guaranteed fundamental freedoms in Section 2 of the Charter or a conflict with the legal rights in Sections 7 to 15 of the Charter. This method of infringing Charter rights does not appear to be attractive to Parliament or the provincial legislatures, in part as a result of the political unpopularity of such a declaration.

q. RESTRICTION IN THE USE OF ILLEGALLY OBTAINED EVIDENCE

The new Constitution changes the traditional rule in Canada that police could use illegally obtained evidence against an accused person in a criminal trial. Where evidence is obtained by violating constitutional rights, such as through an illegal search or by violating the right of an arrested person to consult a lawyer without delay, the court can now exclude such evidence from the trial where its use would "bring the administration of justice into disrepute."

r. OTHER REMEDIES FOR VIOLATION OF CIVIL RIGHTS

The Charter provides as follows:

> 24.(1) Anyone whose rights or freedoms, as guaranteed by this Charter, have been infringed or denied may apply to a court of competent jurisdiction to obtain such remedy as the court considers appropriate and just in the circumstances.

This is a new constitutional source of remedy that can be used for violations of constitutional rights. Significant remedies have been used by some courts dealing with violations of constitutional rights including staying the proceedings against the accused, dismissing charges, and rejecting evidence where it has been obtained illegally. The new laws will have to be interpreted by the courts for many years before the rules become clearly defined. The range of remedies is discussed in more detail in chapter 34.

s. THE STATUS OF OUR NEW CONSTITUTIONAL RIGHTS

Traditionally, civil rights in Canada did not have constitutional protection. Such rights were protected by the common law and the Canadian Bill of Rights, but it was always possible for Parliament to pass a law restricting or violating our basic rights.

Now these rights are protected in a constitution. Section 52 of the Constitution Act provides that the Constitution, including the Charter of Rights and Freedoms, is the supreme law of Canada and any law that is inconsistent with the provisions of the Constitution is, to the extent of the inconsistency, of no force or effect. This means the Constitution overrides any law that is inconsistent with it. Many challenges are being made to existing laws on the basis that they violate some of the constitutional rights.

2
THE RIGHTS OF SUSPECTS

The situations in which police have a lawful right to stop and detain you are very limited in Canadian law. Police may stop any person they consider to be suspicious. A police officer is allowed to walk up to a person in the street and to ask questions just as any stranger can.

There is no restriction whatever on a police officer's right to ask questions. However, no officer has the right to detain you without a legal reason. This means, for example, that if an officer walks up to you, confronts you, and begins to ask questions without stating a legal reason for doing so, you can walk away without answering any of the questions.

a. THE GENERAL RULES: THE RIGHT TO REMAIN SILENT

There are a few general rules that govern the citizen's relations with police. The primary rule is the right to remain silent.

No person is required to answer questions asked by police officers. Certainly a police officer is entitled to ask questions, but no one is required to answer.

No law in Canada requires police officers to tell a suspect of the right to remain silent. If you are a suspect, you are not under arrest, and police are not required to advise you of your right to retain and instruct a lawyer without delay. Nor are they required to warn you that any statements you make may be used against you at a subsequent trial.

The law says the police should warn an arrested person prior to interrogating him or her, although a judge may permit the statements of an accused person to be used in evidence despite the absence of a warning.

b. THE RIGHT TO COUNSEL

You have an absolute right to consult with a lawyer if you have been arrested or detained by police in Canada. A person who is not under arrest can demand that the police allow him or her freedom to leave and can go to a lawyer's office.

For example, a suspect can invoke this right when police officers arrive to question him or her. It is perfectly permissible to ask the police what the subject matter of their visit is, to advise them that you wish to consult with a lawyer before answering questions, and to terminate the interview.

Since April 17, 1982, under the Charter of Rights and Freedoms, police in Canada are required to tell an arrested or detained person about the right to retain and instruct counsel without delay. It is an express constitutional right to be so advised. Failure of police to do this may result in dismissal of the charge or rejection of evidence obtained following the illegal arrest.

In the case of a person who is under arrest, police officers must permit sufficient phone calls to contact a lawyer either at the time of the arrest or after being booked at the police station.

c. THE RIGHT TO A TELEPHONE CALL

The right of a person in police custody to telephone a lawyer is part of the right to counsel. There is no specific restriction on the number of phone calls that are allowed, although it must be reasonable and involve a *bona fide* attempt to contact counsel. An arrested person who does not know a lawyer may wish to contact a relative or friend to find a lawyer, or to consult a legal aid office.

d. ADMISSIONS AND CONFESSIONS

Many people are convicted of criminal offences by evidence that comes out of their own mouth. Many cases would never reach the court if an accused person had not made incriminating statements, either admissions of some fact which the police needed to prove, or confessions of the commission of a crime.

The cardinal rule for a suspect or an arrested person is that it is always better to discuss the circumstances with a lawyer of his or her choice before granting interviews to the police. Some people make statements as a result of intimidation or fear set up by the police; it is in precisely such situations that the suspect or arrested person should demand the opportunity to contact counsel.

It is extremely unwise to make false statements to the police, and this practice frequently backfires on suspects. The police are often in a position to prove many details of a case before they come to interview the suspect. They may be in a position to prove that certain statements made to them are, in fact, dishonest. Even if you are innocent, you could convict yourself in court on the basis of dishonest statements to police.

A judge or jury hearing the trial will form a negative view of an accused person where police are able to show that that person has attempted to mislead them. It may also be a criminal offence to mislead police in the course of an investigation. You are very seldom going to assist yourself by lying to the police. More commonly, you will unwittingly provide evidence that will make the police case against you more complete.

e. ORAL STATEMENTS TO POLICE

A common misconception is the belief that a suspect's statement must be in writing before it can be used against him or her. This is not true.

In law, any incriminating statement, whether made orally or in writing, may be used in evidence against an accused person. A statement may arise in casual conversation during a lull in activities of the police investigation, or it may be a statement made to some other person, such as a relative, in the presence of police. Any statement made to a booking desk officer or to a custodial sheriff or guard may be used as evidence.

As for written statements, it does not matter whether the suspect writes the statement out or whether the police officer writes the statement out and the suspect signs it. As long as you adopt the writing as your statement, it may be offered in evidence against you.

f. WHAT MAKES A PERSON A SUSPECT?

There is no simple answer to this question. Normally, the police will already have uncovered a trail of evidence that points to the suspect.

This trail of evidence may include eye witnesses, circumstantial evidence, wire-tap evidence, evidence of informers or accomplices (former associates of the suspect who have reached a bargain with police or prosecutors), physical evidence (fingerprints, hair, clothing, paint chips, identifying marks found at the scene of a crime), and so on.

Anyone who becomes a suspect in the course of a police investigation will be contacted. Initial contact from police while they are still investigating a case may take the form of a visit to the home or office, with or without a search warrant. (See chapters 7, 8, 9, 13, 16, 17, and 22, dealing with search warrants.)

Generally, though not always, police attendance with a search warrant will be a strong indication that the investigation is leading definitely to the suspect. The issuance of a search warrant shows that a justice of the peace was satisfied that there were reasonable grounds for believing the suspect had committed an offence. Circumstances where the grounds for granting a search warrant were inadequate are discussed in the various chapters dealing with search warrants.

In other cases, it may be sheer speculation on the part of police that the suspect may know something about the case. The object is, in part, to obtain information that may be incriminating to the suspect and to build a case for prosecution. Sometimes the police may be on a fishing expedition, hoping to get information that will lead them in a fruitful direction.

g. POLICE AT YOUR RESIDENCE, OFFICE, OR WORKPLACE

If police officers come to your home, it may be a bitter and embarrassing experience. It may be upsetting to your spouse and children or other family members.

The police do not have the right to search the house unless they have a search warrant. They do not have the right to take the suspect to the police station unless they decide to arrest and charge him or her. The suspect has the right to contact a lawyer.

In the case of arrest, it may be wise to phone your lawyer from home before leaving for the police station. You have a constitutional right to retain and instruct counsel without delay. The exercise of this right would enable your lawyer to arrive at the police station at about the same time you arrive and would facilitate a speedy consultation. In the meantime, before talking to your lawyer, it is almost invariably better to remain silent.

h. THE BASIC RULES OF SEARCH AND SEIZURE

The general rule is that police or other official investigators are not entitled to search a place unless they have a search warrant. Any person in control of property, as owner, supervisor, manager, or in some other capacity, has the right to object to and prevent any unlawful search of premises or seizure of documents. Illegal seizure of property by police may lead to civil actions or criminal charges, such as theft and possession, against them.

A further fundamental rule is that there can be no search of a "dwelling-house" without a search warrant or written statutory authorization. This is the common law principle that "a man's home is his castle." Dwelling-house is defined as the whole or part of any building or structure kept or occupied as a permanent residence. It includes a rented room, apartment, or mobile home.

The dwelling-house is no longer so inviolate as were the castles of earlier times with their moats and private armies; however, the principle remains a basic rule of Canadian law. There are now many statutes that provide for the issuing of search warrants to permit a search of private dwellings, but proper grounds must exist for a justice to grant the search warrant. Each warrant is valid only for a particular search.

The exceptions to the general rules of search and seizure apply to "places" that are not dwelling-houses, such as vehicles, offices, buildings, and so on. Before referring to the exceptions to the general rule, it is appropriate to mention some legal first aid in cases of illegal search. Some or all of the following steps could be taken:

(a) Advise police that since they have no search warrant, you take the position that the search is unlawful.

(b) Telephone your lawyer.

(c) Ask the lawyer to speak to the police officer in charge.

(d) Ask the lawyer or an associate to come to your premises if feasible.

(e) Obtain the names and badge numbers of officers participating in the unlawful search if the search proceeds.

(f) Record the documents seized, if any.

(g) Meet with counsel as soon as possible after the unlawful entry so that complaints can be laid with the appropriate authorities and civil actions against the officers can be considered.

i. SOME EXCEPTIONS TO THE GENERAL RULES ON SEARCH AND SEIZURE

There are a few important exceptions to the general rule that a search warrant is always required. These exceptions include the following:

(a) A search of a "disorderly house" where illegal gambling is occurring may be carried out by police without a warrant; any documents to support a gambling charge may be seized (see chapter 8).

(b) Under the narcotics laws, a search without warrant is allowed of any place that is not a residence. Police can also search any person found in such place. These laws require the police to have a "reasonable belief" that there are illegal drugs in such a place (see chapter 8).

(c) Under the Food and Drugs Act, a search is allowed without warrant of a place that is not a dwelling-house on the basis of a reasonable belief that there is a controlled (amphetamines, barbiturates, etc.) or restricted (LSD, MDA, Psilocybin, etc.) drug involved in an offence which as been committed. Officers can search any person found in the premises and seize any drugs or other evidence (see chapter 12).

(d) Under the Criminal Code, a search for weapons without a warrant is allowed of any person, vehicle, place, or premises that is not a dwelling-house where police believe illegal guns or other weapons may be found. This law requires that the police have a belief "on reasonable grounds" that a Criminal Code weapons offence has been committed. Police are entitled to seize any weapons found and can hold them for up to three months without laying a charge (see chapter 21).

(e) Examination of records by auditors in the course of routine investigation under the Income Tax Act may be done without a warrant. However, documents may no longer be seized by an auditor in the absence of a search warrant (see chapter 9).

(f) A search of vehicles or vessels for illegal contraband or unlawfully imported goods by police or customs officers under the Customs Act may be carried out without a warrant provided the officers have "reasonable grounds of suspicion." This may lead to seizure of the goods and vehicle (see chapter 17).

(g) A search of a building by customs officers without a warrant is allowed if they are prepared to swear on oath that they have "reasonable cause to suspect" that illegal goods will be found (see chapter 18).

(h) Search without warrant is allowed under provincial liquor laws of any place other than a dwelling-house on the basis of a suspicion that liquor is being kept for an unlawful purpose (see chapter 16).

(i) Under provincial securities legislation, a search without warrant is allowed for documents where it "appears probable" that a person or company has contravened the laws dealing with securities trading.

The person appointed may search for and seize documents, records, or securities of the company or person being investigated.

There are other exceptions or partial exceptions to the general rule. There are eight more chapters of this book dealing specifically with search and seizure setting out some of the exceptions in detail.

j. SEARCH OF PERSON

No one is required to submit to a search of his or her person unless the police officer has a lawful reason for making a search or the person is under arrest.

Section 8 of the Charter of Rights and Freedoms provides that "everyone has the right to be secure against unreasonable search or seizure." If there are no grounds for making a search, it will be found to be unreasonable.

Even if evidence is found, if there were no reason for the search in the first place, a court may reject the evidence on the basis that it may bring the administration of justice into disrepute. Such refusal to permit prosecutors to use the evidence in court is a remedy available under Section 24(2) of the Charter.

If a person is not arrested, the officer must state some other lawful reason for search, such as a belief that the person is illegally carrying drugs, liquor, or weapons.

You are entitled to resist an illegal search, but it is usually more appropriate to inform the officer that you believe the search is illegal and you do not consent to it. If the officer persists, you may sue in civil law for damages for assault, false arrest, or detention, or charge the officer with common assault under criminal law. The risk of this possibility may deter a police officer who is about to proceed with an unlawful personal search.

Note: In extraordinary situations, such as when the War Measures Act is invoked, Parliament can give to police the right to arbitrarily stop and question any person at any time. Before the Constitution Act, 1982, in these situations, the Bill of Rights was suspended and civil rights were virtually non-existent. Arbitrary searches of houses and other places could be authorized.

It remains to be seen how the courts will interpret the Charter of Rights and Freedoms. Constitutional challenges to the validity of the War Measures Act could be made under the Charter.

k. CAN A PERSON BE ARRESTED FOR INVESTIGATION?

Under Section 9 of the Charter of Rights and Freedoms, everyone has a constitutional right not to be arbitrarily detained or imprisoned. If a person is not under arrest, he or she is not required to submit to custody and cannot be held for investigation. If you are under arrest, you are either charged with an offence, or about to be charged. If you are held for investigation, you are not under arrest and are entitled to your freedom.

If police request a suspect to go with them for further investigation, and the suspect agrees to do so, then such "detention" is not unlawful. That is, you can consent to being held without an arrest. It is up to you; but you are not obliged to go. Obviously, if police officers believe there is evidence to support their suspicions, you will be arrested immediately and charged.

It is in cases where the evidence does not justify an arrest on the spot, but where police wish to investigate further, that a suspect may be requested to go to the police station for further investigation. This is not an arrest, and you need not obey such a request.

1. BE DIPLOMATIC

It is always a good policy to try to be polite to police officers. If you are not under arrest, and you do not wish to answer any questions, you are entitled to go on your way. Be as pleasant as possible under the circumstances. You may also find it necessary to be firm.

Police officers in major cities are obliged to carry their badge numbers with them at all times, and it is by the badge number that a particular officer can be identified. You have the right to demand to see the badge in order to satisfy yourself that the person is, in fact, a police officer. If you feel your rights are not being respected, you should ask for the badge number and for the police officer's name.

m. POWERS OF POLICE OFFICERS

Police are protected by law when they are acting lawfully. If they are doing something that they are authorized by law to do, such as making a legal arrest, they are justified in using as much force as is necessary to accomplish their purpose. They are protected provided they have acted on reasonable and probable grounds.

Police are allowed to use force in making an arrest if the arrest cannot be done by reasonable means in a less violent manner. They are also entitled to use handcuffs to prevent the possible escape of people in custody.

In the past, practices such as choking a person suspected of having a narcotic have been held justifiable on the grounds that a police officer was entitled to make an oral search on the basis of a reasonable belief that the accused was carrying a narcotic in his or her mouth. This law was criticized on the basis that simple possession of a narcotic for personal use is generally a summary offence and does not carry heavy penalties, and the procedures employed are dangerous to the suspect's health and potentially life threatening.

This type of choke hold search has been successfully challenged on the basis that it violates the right of a person to be secure against unreasonable search or seizure. The Supreme Court of Canada decided that the appropriate remedy in this circumstance was to exclude the evidence thereby illegally obtained.

n. POLICE IN A PUBLIC PLACE: WHAT WILL AROUSE SUSPICION?

Some people have the unfortunate ability to appear suspicious to police officers even when they are not involved in any illegal activity. To some extent, this depends entirely on the personality of the particular police officer involved. Some police officers, for example, may consider it suspicious for any young person to be out at 3:00 a.m. Other police officers will not consider this to be suspicious unless the person is walking down an alley behind business premises where there would be an opportunity for breaking and entering.

Similarly, some officers will be suspicious of people walking in a skid road area in which drugs are commonly available, or under-age youths lurking about a liquor store or licenced premises. An extraordinarily disheveled appearance, tattoos, motorcycles, or anything of that sort may strike some police officers as suspicious.

The number of potentially suspicious circumstances is infinite and each situation depends entirely on its own facts and the participants involved. The only generalization that can be made is that a suspicious circumstance may be any situation in which an officer may regard your appearance or behavior as irregular. Nevertheless, a good knowledge of your civil rights will help you handle the situation if you are stopped by the police.

o. REASONS FOR STOPPING PEOPLE IN PUBLIC PLACES

Canada no longer has the type of vagrancy laws that allow police to stop people routinely and question them as to their means of support and place of residence.

However, police on patrol commonly stop people under the cover of drug, weapons, or liquor laws. These laws are sufficiently vague to allow police officers to stop people and search someone on a *reasonable* suspicion that the suspects might have illegal drugs, weapons, or alcohol.

The reasonableness of an officer's grounds for stopping you and questioning or searching you under these laws is difficult to determine and not generally something that can be determined on the spur of the moment with any degree of rationality. The statutes themselves do not set out any criteria for determining these things.

The new constitutional protection in Section 8 of the Charter against unreasonable search or seizure will be important in these areas. As legal cases under the Charter are decided, the courts will develop standards of what constitutes unreasonable search or seizure.

As a general rule, if an officer stops you for no apparent reason and begins to ask questions, you do not have to answer. The law does not require you even to identify yourself or supply any information unless the officer has a legal reason for making such a request. Where a legal reason is given, it may be a legal reason for stopping you, but not for asking questions. It will probably not be a reason to request you to answer questions, unless you are a driver of a motor vehicle being stopped under provincial driving laws.

Formerly, the vagrancy law allowed police to stop and question any suspicious-looking persons. Vagrancy was a summary offence under the Criminal Code and included the charge of wandering or trespassing with no apparent means of support and failing to justify one's presence to a police officer when required to do so.

It enabled an officer to stop you anywhere and demand that you justify your presence. There was no right to remain silent because failure to provide an explanation could be used as evidence. This was one of the common means for stopping suspicious people in public places.

Under present laws, investigation of drugs, weapons, and liquor offences is a common reason for police to stop and question people in public places. In municipalities where a curfew is in effect, this may be a ground for police to stop and question young people.

Some laws are inherently vague and may possibly lend themselves to abuse. For example, the charge of causing a disturbance can be interpreted in a number of different ways to cover any number of situations. A man standing on a sidewalk in such a manner that others must walk around him in order to continue on their way might arguably be causing a disturbance by loitering and obstructing or by impeding. Shouting or swearing in a public place may amount to causing a disturbance.

Police are generally busy with legitimate investigations and patrols and do not set out to harass individuals. Most of us will never experience police harassment. However, there are known examples where abuse or harassment by a police officer has occurred. In those situations, these general rules always apply:

(a) If you are not under arrest, you are entitled to go on your way.

(b) There is no right to search without giving a legal reason.

(c) No one stopped in a public place is required to answer questions.

p. DRIVERS

Provincial motor vehicle laws authorize police to stop any motor vehicle and ask the driver to produce his or her driver's licence, vehicle registration, and insurance evidence. If you drive a vehicle, always be prepared to produce these three documents. You may also be asked the name and address of the driver and owner of the vehicle. The police have no right to question passengers unless one of the passengers happens to also be the owner. Then the police can make only the requests listed above.

If the police try to search the car, ask to see a search warrant. If they inform you they are searching under the drugs, weapons, or liquor laws, they may have the right to proceed without a warrant if they have grounds. Otherwise, they have no right to search a vehicle without a warrant and you may resist the search, using such force as is reasonably necessary in the circumstances to resist the search successfully.

If police detain you to take a breathalyzer test or arrest you for impaired driving with the same intent, you must be told of your right to consult with a lawyer without delay.

Any person arrested or detained has the right under the Constitution to retain and instruct counsel without delay. Police must make a telephone available for this purpose. In addition, police must provide private space for the person so that lawyer/client confidentiality can be maintained.

q. INVESTIGATION OF DRINKING AND DRIVING CASES

Possible drinking and driving offences are common reasons for stopping motor vehicles. If police have reasonable and probable grounds for believing that an offence of impaired driving or driving with more than 80 milligrams of alcohol per 100 millilitres of blood has been committed, they can demand that the driver accompany them and supply at least two samples of breath for analysis (see chapter 15 where this is discussed in greater detail).

This does not necessarily involve an arrest, although police commonly arrest for impaired driving offences if they have decided to demand breath tests. A suspect has the right to refuse to answer questions, except those dealing with motor vehicle registration, insurance, and driver's licence documents.

A person who has been detained or arrested has the right to consult with a lawyer before taking a breathalyzer test. The duty is no longer on the accused person to assert that right. The police officer must advise the suspect of the right to retain counsel, and provide an opportunity for that suspect to contact counsel. Otherwise the right under Section 10(b) of the Charter would be a hollow right. There are a number of cases in which the courts have ruled there has been a Charter breach on the basis that the detained person has been denied a full opportunity to reach counsel, or has been interrupted in his conversation with counsel, or asked to provide a breath sample before making contact with counsel.

3
THE LAW OF ARREST

a. SUMMARY AND INDICTABLE OFFENCES: WHAT'S THE DIFFERENCE?

The powers of arrest of police officers are different for summary and indictable offences. Generally, summary offences are minor types of charges and carry lesser maximum penalties. They are similar to misdemeanor offences in the United States. An indictable offence is more serious, carries heavier penalties, and is similar to a felony in the United States.

Many offences may be tried either summarily or by indictment, at the option of the prosecutors. Offences that may be either summary *or* indictable include possession of narcotics, offences under the Food and Drugs Act, offences under the Income Tax Act, and Criminal Code charges such as impaired driving and assault.

These optional charges must be treated for most purposes as indictable. (For other important differences between summary and indictable proceedings, see chapter 5 on booking procedures and chapter 31 on criminal records.)

b. INDICTABLE OFFENCES

Some offences are always indictable. These include charges of theft, possession, false pretenses or fraud when the value of what is obtained is *over* $1 000, charges of forgery, breaking and entering, breaking out of jail, perjury, treason, sedition, and all other very serious offences.

Most weapons charges may be summary or indictable on the option of the prosecutor. Some weapons offences are only indictable, such as possession of a weapon for a purpose dangerous to the public peace.

Sexual assaults may be summary or indictable, however, sexual assault with a weapon or aggravated sexual assault is always indictable.

c. SUMMARY OFFENCES

Summary offences include the Criminal Code charges of causing a disturbance, unlawful assembly, nudity in a public place, and soliciting for the purpose of prostitution. Infractions of all municipal and provincial enactments, such as hitch-hiking and jaywalking laws, noise by-laws, motor vehicle offences, and liquor charges, are summary offences.

You can be arrested for a summary offence if you are found committing it, or on the basis of a warrant that has been issued for your arrest.

d. THE ARREST

In order to make a lawful arrest, the arresting officer should identify himself or herself, state that you are under arrest, and touch you to indicate that you are in custody. You *must* be informed of the reason for the arrest or be shown the warrant where it is feasible to do so. (For example, it isn't feasible if you are running from a bank with a gun in one hand and a mask and pillow case in the other. In this case, the reason for the arrest is obvious!)

In the case of indictable offences (which includes offences that may be summary or indictable), the police have wider powers of arrest. You can be arrested if you have committed an indictable offence or if the officer *believes* on *reasonable and probable grounds*, that you have committed or are about to commit an indictable offence.

If you are about to commit an indictable offence and are arrested, but not charged with attempting to commit the offence, you must be released as soon as the officers are satisfied there is no longer a risk that you will commit the offence.

e. CONSTITUTIONAL RIGHTS AT THE TIME OF ARREST

There are important new constitutional rights since the Charter of Rights and Freedoms became law.

First, an arrested or detained person has the right to be advised by police of his or her right to retain and instruct counsel without delay. Failure to do so will make the arrest an unlawful one.

In addition, an arrested or detained person has an express constitutional right to contact counsel without delay. Police must provide the opportunity to do this and the opportunity to speak with counsel in private.

Since the proclamation of the Charter, the scope of what constitutes detention by the police has widened considerably. It now is the law that when a person is stopped by a police officer and asked questions in the course of an investigation, and that person is not free to leave the company of the police officer, he or she is considered to have been detained. It is at this point of detention that a person's Charter rights arise. It is important to note at what point exactly the police officer advises of the right to counsel.

f. ILLEGAL ARRESTS

In Canada, it is legal to refuse to comply with the attempts of a police officer to make an illegal arrest. You may use as much force as is reasonably necessary to escape the officer's grasp. This isn't encouraged, as there may be great difficulty in making an instant decision about whether the arrest is legal or illegal. (In some states in the United States "no-sock" laws make it an offence to resist an illegal arrest. You can be guilty of violating a no-sock law even if you merely go limp and resist passively.)

Resisting an illegal arrest can be hazardous as it may result in a charge of assaulting or obstructing a police officer. If the arrest is illegal, you would have a defence to these charges; but if you do not have witnesses, there is a danger that your testimony may not be accepted in court and you could be convicted.

The general rules in Canadian law is that the offence of resisting arrest requires an act of resistance, and passive resistance, such as going limp, does not constitute resistance.

No person is entitled to interfere with a police officer who is carrying out his or her duty in arresting another person. If you are in a situation in which an associate is being arrested and you are on the scene, you must not interfere or obstruct the police officer. You are entitled to remain present to observe the arrest, but cannot interfere.

Obstructing a police officer is an offence under the Criminal Code. If you are so charged, you can be convicted if the police officer can show that he or she was performing the duties of a police officer and was obstructed by you.

g. CITIZEN'S ARREST

Any citizen, including a store detective or a private security officer, has a limited power of arrest. He or she may arrest a person found committing an indictable offence, or a person believed, on reasonable and probable grounds, to be committing a criminal offence and being chased by police.

A citizen who makes an arrest is under an obligation to deliver the arrested person forthwith to a police officer. This means that he or she must turn the arrested person over to police as soon as possible. Failure to do this makes the arrest illegal, and the arrested person may sue for damages.

By far the most common form of citizen's arrest occurs in cases of theft under $1 000, commonly referred to as shoplifting. Store detectives can arrest a person on the basis of mere suspicion that the person has shoplifted. They have no right to search and must turn the arrested person over to the police immediately.

If you are innocent of shoplifting you may resist the arrest by a store detective using such force as is necessary to obtain your freedom. Sometimes it may be wiser to follow another course. If you object verbally to the arrest and are later released, or acquitted of the charge, you can bring a civil suit against the particular store detective and against the store itself for damages for assault, defamation of character, false imprisonment, and malicious prosecution.

h. CHARGED BUT NOT ARRESTED

Under certain circumstances a police officer will charge you without making an arrest. The police are not required to arrest a person charged with the following matters:

(a) A summary offence (such as causing a disturbance)//
(b) An offence that may be summary or indictable (such as possession of marijuana)
(c) An offence that must be tried by a magistrate (such as theft, possession, or false pretenses or fraud where the value is under $1 000)

The test that the police officer is required by law to apply is whether or not it is in the public interest to make the arrest.

If the officer doesn't need to arrest you to establish your identity, to secure or preserve evidence of the offence, to prevent the continuation or repetition of the crime, or the commission of another crime, he or she has a discretion to release you on the spot.

However, the officer will issue an appearance notice stating that you must attend court on a certain date. Where the offence is indictable or may be indictable, the notice will state that you must attend at a certain time and place for fingerprinting and photographing. This matter is dealt with more fully in the chapters dealing with bail law (see chapters 23, 24, and 25).

The police officer can refuse to release you if there is a danger you will fail to attend court when required. A police officer cannot release the accused if the offence is indictable and was committed in another province.

The power of police officers to release by an appearance notice in these types of cases is obviously a good reason to treat them courteously whenever possible. It is obviously much more convenient from the accused's point of view not to be arrested.

In some areas of Canada, a person arrested on a Friday evening, and not released by police, may remain in custody until Monday morning, which may be the earliest time that a justice of the peace, magistrate, or provincial court judge is available.

4
THE CONSEQUENCES OF AN ARREST

Once you have been legally arrested, your situation changes markedly. The police have the power to search you and will usually do so. They will frisk you on the street and then take you to the station where you will be booked, a process that consists of taking your personal belongings from you, including perhaps your belt and shoelaces.

At this stage you will be asked for details such as your name, address, and date of birth; your condition and any visible scars may be noted by police officers. You will likely be searched again and, in some cases, where there is cause to believe you might have drugs on your person, you may be stripped and skin-frisked.

a. THE RIGHT TO REMAIN SILENT AFTER AN ARREST

The right to remain silent and the right not to incriminate yourself continues throughout every stage of the criminal justice process.

You are not obliged to answer police questions, even at the booking desk. However, the questions asked by the booking officer are normally harmless. Apart from these questions and questions by an officer in charge relating to bail, it is a good practice to refuse to answer any questions until after you have had a chance to consult a lawyer.

Upon arrest, police must warn you of the reasons for the arrest. They should also warn you that you need not make any statements, but that anything you do say may be taken down and used in evidence against you. However, this warning regarding statements is not a legal requirement in Canada.

If you are not warned, and you make incriminating statements, a judge may find your statements inadmissible as evidence against you. The judge will look at the circumstances of the arrest and interrogation in deciding whether to throw out a confession. The failure of police to give a warning is only one factor that the judge will consider.

Whether or not you are warned about making statements, the best advice is to remain silent until you have consulted with a lawyer. You may tell an officer that you have nothing to say until you have had the opportunity to speak with counsel.

b. IS SILENCE ALWAYS WISE?

There may be instances in which you do not wish to remain silent. You may be innocent of the charge, or you may know that the police have arrested the wrong person. In these circumstances, it may be useful to tell them so immediately and offer an explanation or alibi concerning the offence for which you are being arrested.

Certainly a judge is more inclined to accept your alibi if it was offered at the first opportunity, but you should be sure of your facts before you state where you were at the time of the alleged offence. However, it is much safer to make any statement through a lawyer, or at least after consulting with a lawyer.

It is also advantageous to make a statement if you are arrested for possession of stolen property. The arresting officer will demand that you explain how you came to be in possession of the property. If you didn't know the goods were stolen, the police should be told this. The fact that you gave an explanation at the time of arrest will weigh in your favor in court. If you received the goods in circumstances that now strike you as suspicious, you may wish to tell the officer you will happily make a statement after consulting a lawyer.

One curious bit of law in Canada refers to the charge of possession of instruments suitable for the purpose of housebreaking, vault-breaking, or safe-breaking. The law formerly read that police could charge anyone who was in possession of a screwdriver or other instrument in a situation that aroused the officer's suspicions.

It has been reformed a little, but is still subject to misuse by law enforcement officers. The way the law reads now, anyone who is in possession of an instrument (e.g., a screwdriver), under circumstances that cause a police officer to make a reasonable inference that the instrument is or was being used for housebreaking, vault-breaking, or safe-breaking, can be arrested and charged with the offence.

The accused is presumed to be guilty unless he or she can establish a lawful excuse for being in possession of the instrument under the circumstances. There are very few cases under this section and nothing to indicate what will be considered as circumstances giving rise to a reasonable inference that the instrument was used or is being used for the purpose of housebreaking. If you are observed by a police officer late at night with a screwdriver or any similar tool in your possession, and you are in an area in which housebreaking or related offences recently occurred, you can be arrested for possession of instruments for the purpose of housebreaking.

Should this happen, you may wish to explain why you have the screwdriver or other implement in your possession.

If the explanation satisfies the officer, you may not be charged. Again, it is safer to consult with a lawyer before giving the explanation.

Finally, a youth who is entitled to be dealt with in youth court should immediately tell police his or her age. In youth court, there is greater emphasis on the special needs and rehabilitation of the accused. Sometimes no charges are laid or proceeded with or interim release is granted. There is also a general emphasis against incarceration as a penalty.

In some cases in which youths have lied about their age, and were therefore charged in adult court, the appellate courts have held that conviction should stand even though the adult court would never have jurisdiction in the first instance if the youths had given the correct age.

5
BOOKED, FINGERPRINTED, AND PHOTOGRAPHED

We have seen that police have a right to search a person they have arrested. They will search for weapons that might be used to assist an escape or to commit suicide, or for evidence relating to the charge.

This search may occur at the time of arrest or at the time of booking, and it sometimes includes a skin-frisk if narcotics are suspected to be hidden on the person. If, during this search, evidence is found (e.g., drugs or a weapon) that will support a completely unrelated charge, the additional charge will normally be laid.

a. DON'T TALK ABOUT YOUR CHARGE

At the booking desk, the booking officer will take your personal possessions and will ask you to sign a paper listing them. He or she may chat about your arrest and may ask questions, but you are not required to talk or to answer the questions.

An impaired driver may be questioned about the amount he or she has had to drink, or about any medical or health conditions that may cause blood-shot eyes or slurred speech or an unsteady walk. These kinds of statements can be used against the accused at the trial.

Any police officer to whom you make an incriminating statement may be called as a witness against you. It is a good rule of thumb to speak with a lawyer before making any statement that has a remote chance of being incriminating or misconstrued. If you want to be friendly, talk about the weather or the working conditions of police officers. It is *not* a good idea to discuss the charge pending against you.

Informers or "stool pigeons" are sometimes planted in cells with people freshly arrested. This is a sure-fire method of getting voluntary confessions. Prisoners often chat about what they're in for; some like to boast about their particular exploit. An inflated boast to an undercover officer could convict an innocent accused. It may also add to the seriousness of an otherwise fairly mild offence. For your own self-preservation, you should be friendly to cell-mates, but *don't* talk about your case.

b. YOUR RIGHT TO A BAIL HEARING

The Constitution gives a person charged with an offence the right "not to be denied reasonable bail without just cause."

Even after an arrest, the police can release you on bail in all but the most serious of cases. Again, if they do not do so, you have the right to appear within 24 hours, or as soon thereafter as possible, before a justice, magistrate, or provincial court judge for a bail hearing. These matters are dealt with extensively in chapters 23, 24, and 25.

c. YOUR RIGHT TO COUNSEL

Once you are in custody, you must be advised of the right to retain and instruct counsel without delay. You have the right to make telephone calls to notify relatives and obtain counsel. Your right to counsel is a constitutional right that police may not deny.

You must be given a reasonable opportunity to contact a lawyer of your choice. This usually means giving you access to a telephone and sufficient privacy so that you can consult with your lawyer without being overheard by any police officers. It also means being able to make as many telephone calls as are reasonably necessary to contact a lawyer.

If you think that you have been improperly arrested, there is very little point in complaining to the police who have made the arrest, and there is no point in bringing it to the attention of the jail guards.

It is much more sensible to request a telephone call to a lawyer and to tell him or her about the situation. The lawyer may be able to contact a prosecutor or a justice of the peace to arrange a judicial interim release for you.

d. RIGHT TO BE INFORMED OF THE SPECIFIC CHARGE AGAINST YOU

Under Section 10(a) of the Charter, a person who is arrested or detained has the right to be "informed promptly of the reasons therefor."

A person who has actually been charged with an offence has the right "to be informed without unreasonable delay of the specific offence." As suggested earlier, unreasonable delay might be considered to be 24 hours.

e. HOW LONG ARE YOU KEPT IN CUSTODY?

In large urban centres, a justice of the peace is usually on duty 24 hours a day, seven days a week. These justices are not provincial court judges or magistrates, but they have powers to release an accused person for any but the most serious offences. Often, however, they are reluctant to do so where there is a criminal record or unusually serious circumstances.

Unfortunately, in more rural areas, there are often no provincial court judges or magistrates sitting or available on Saturday or Sunday. This means that if you are arrested late Friday evening, you may, in a serious matter, be kept in custody until Monday morning, when your detention is reviewed by a judge.

If you are arrested on the grounds that you are *about* to commit an indictable offence, you will be released unconditionally, once the police are satisfied that you will not commit the offence. If they do not release you, then you must be taken before a justice of the peace, provincial court judge, or magistrate within 24 hours or as soon as possible.

f. FINGERPRINTS AND PHOTOGRAPHS

The Identification of Criminals Act gives police a right to fingerprint and photograph persons charged with an indictable offence. They may use force if necessary. It should be remembered that many drug and weapons charges may be either summary or indictable at the option of the prosecutor. All these offences should be treated as indictable.

If you resist fingerprinting and photographing on a charge such as possession of marijuana, the prosecutor may decide to proceed by indictable offence if for no other reason than to protect the police who may have forcibly fingerprinted and photographed you.

Where you are charged with a summary offence, police have no right to take fingerprints and photographs. You are entitled to resist. If the police use force, you may sue civilly for damages or lay a charge of assault.

If you are released on an appearance notice, promise to appear, or recognizance, you can be required to appear at a specified time and place for fingerprinting and photographing. If you do not appear at the time and place specified, a warrant can be issued for your arrest for the offence with which you are charged. This means that the form of bail that is in effect will be cancelled, and you will be held in custody, unless there is a new undertaking, promise to appear, or recognizance. You can also be charged with failing to appear for fingerprinting and photographing.

6
FURTHER RIGHTS OF AN ACCUSED PERSON

The material in this chapter again presupposes that a person has been arrested on a specific charge, although he or she may not yet have appeared in court.

To recapitulate, police have no right to hold anyone for investigation, for questioning, or on the basis of suspicion unless they are prepared to make a formal arrest for a specific offence. However, if a person under investigation consents to the custody then there is no actual imprisonment.

The suspect who is not under arrest must assert his or her right to be free. Police have no obligation to tell you about your right to retain and instruct counsel unless you have been arrested or detained. It is sometimes difficult to determine if you are being detained or merely questioned by the police.

The real issue is whether you are free to leave at a given moment. A person who is not free to leave is detained. The courts are increasingly widening the scope as to what constitutes detention and defining at precisely what moment a person is detained by a police officer.

A person who is arrested or detained must be told of the right to retain and instruct counsel without delay. You have that right and are entitled to exercise it. Police must give a person in custody reasonable opportunity for obtaining counsel. They must provide a telephone, a telephone directory, and private space to consult with counsel.

As stated in chapter 5, police are entitled to search you, to take your belongings, to book you and, if you are in custody for an indictable offence, to fingerprint and photograph you.

Beyond this, there are several requests that police may make to an arrested person in the course of their investigation, but the arrested person is not required to comply with these requests. Indeed, if any of the requests discussed below are made by police, you should consult with counsel before complying.

a. LINE-UPS AND SHOW-UPS

There are two different kinds of identification procedures known as line-ups and show-ups. In a line-up the suspect is placed among a group of persons who theoretically have similar physical characteristics and a witness or the victim is asked to identify the suspect. This may occur before or after a formal arrest.

A show-up is where the witnesses or a victim simply view the suspect standing alone, either in the police station or in some other place. Line-ups are sometimes referred to as identification parades.

There is no requirement under Canadian statute law to enter a line-up or to appear in front of any witnesses. This is probably not a requirement of a detained person under any Canadian law. However, each situation is different, and it is very important for a detained person to contact a lawyer.

There may be some cases where an accused person will have an excellent opportunity to demonstrate innocence by participating in a line-up. If you are asked by police to participate in a line-up, the best tactic is to request contact with a lawyer before participating. The right of a detained person to consult a lawyer without delay always takes priority over any line-up.

In short, you probably have the right not to enter a line-up and you probably have the right to cover your face if there is a show-up. The problem is that there is no exclusionary rule if witnesses pick you out of a manifestly unfair line-up.

A judge will look at all the circumstances, but is entitled to consider the evidence of the identification by the witnesses even if the line-up contained several other persons who all looked substantially different from you.

Unfortunately, many line-ups contain fairly clean-cut police officers and other persons who may have no resemblance to the suspect. The situation may be worse for a Native Indian, Oriental, or other person of different racial extraction. A lone Asian for instance, in a line-up with eight blond Caucasians may mistakenly be picked out by a victim or witness who alleges that the suspect was a non-white.

There is no absolute right to demand a line-up. However, in a trial a judge could probably direct a line-up. It could also be arranged by agreement with Crown counsel prior to trial if your lawyer thought it desirable.

b. SHOWING PHOTOGRAPHS TO WITNESSES

There have been cases in Canadian law where photographs of a suspect were shown to witnesses or victims shortly before a line-up. This has been held to be unfair and improper as it encourages the possible witness to pick out the person shown in the pictures.

There are many situations in which showing photographs to witnesses before trial may be improper. It always depends on the circumstances. Generally, judges have ruled that pictures ought to be shown to witnesses individually, without comment by police officers or other witnesses.

When identification is an issue in the trial, there will normally be an exclusion order, which means that all witnesses except the particular witness who is testifying will be excluded from the court room.

c. POLYGRAPH TESTS

The polygraph or lie-detector is never a required part of a criminal case. You should never under any circumstances agree to take a polygraph test without having the benefit of a lawyer's advice.

There may be circumstances where your lawyer will want you to take a polygraph test. If so, the lawyer will probably agree with Crown counsel and the police that the test be administered under certain specific terms and conditions. These might include the following:

(a) That the test be administered in a mutually agreeable surrounding (perhaps in the office of a private polygraph tester) and that the questions to be put to you be mutually agreed upon between Crown and defence counsel

(b) If it is a favorable result by the suspect on the polygraph test, the Crown will drop any charges or discontinue the investigation

(c) If it is a bad result, indicating possible guilt, no comment will be made on it in any court and that there will be no attempt in future by Crown counsel to lead the evidence of the bad result in any court proceedings

The court must not be involved in decisions or arrangements for an accused to take a polygraph test.

It is a good practice to engage an independent polygraph examiner who is not actively working for the police force. Most independent polygraph testers are ex-police officers, and have extensive experience in performing polygraph tests and interpreting the results.

d. POLICE DEMAND FOR FINGERPRINTS AND PHOTOGRAPHS WHERE ACCUSED NOT CHARGED WITH INDICTABLE OFFENCE

An accused must be charged with an indictable offence before police are legally entitled to fingerprint and photograph him or her. In all other cases the accused is entitled to refuse a request for fingerprints or for a photograph.

e. HANDWRITING SAMPLES

Handwriting analysis is important in many cases. In cases of forgery, fraud, false pretences, and so on, an issue may arise as to whether the handwriting on a potential exhibit is the same handwriting as the accused's.

An accused in custody should never provide handwriting samples without first consulting counsel.

Most of the time, handwriting analysis will be conducted in a fair manner; however, there are always exceptions.

If samples of handwriting are to be provided for comparison and analysis, then counsel for the accused should be involved in this procedure. If the lawyer deems it in the best interest of the accused then samples should be provided.

In major Canadian cities, handwriting analysts are available on a private basis, separate from police agencies. There is frequently a good deal of doubt about the validity of conclusions from handwriting comparison and analysis, and it is often useful for the defence to obtain a second opinion.

f. SAMPLES OF BREATH, URINE, OR BLOOD

Samples of breath or urine may frequently be requested by police to determine the level of alcohol in the body. This can be relevant to intention to commit a crime in the case of a great many offences. Sometimes, it will be in the interest of an accused person to preserve evidence of the state of intoxication, such as where an accused is charged with a major offence like homicide apparently committed under a high degree of intoxication.

The general rule is that you are not required to provide samples of your breath, blood, or urine for alcohol testing except in accordance with the impaired driving laws. Those provisions are dealt with the chapter 15.

There may also be specific laws under motor vehicle legislation enacted by various provinces. If you are stopped and a request for blood, breath, or urine is made under federal criminal laws, or provincial motor vehicles laws, it may be very important to request the opportunity to discuss the matter with legal counsel.

7
TYPES OF PARTICIPATION IN A CRIME

There are several different kinds of activity that may be involved in the commission of a criminal offence. Some of them may not involve any direct or tangible participation in the actual crime.

The following is a general description of the types of participation in crime.

a. PRINCIPALS TO THE OFFENCE AND AIDING AND ABETTING

People who are party to the offence as principals include the person alleged to have actually committed the offence and those who are alleged to have aided, abetted, or assisted any person in committing the offence. As a general rule, this excludes people who are mere passive bystanders, doing nothing to further the offence, even though they may be associates of the principals; however, the line is sometimes a thin one. For example, sometimes a case can be made that the passive person was actually keeping guard or participating in intimidation of the victim where a crime such as assault, robbery, or rape is being alleged.

Encouraging the principal offender in any way during the commission of the offence will make a person a party to the offence.

In certain crimes (e.g., child neglect), mere presence may constitute the offence. The Criminal Code creates an offence for any parent, foster parent, guardian, or head of a family who fails to provide necessaries of life for a child under the age of 16 if such omission endangers the life of the child or causes or is likely to cause damage to the health of the child.

b. JOINT COMMISSION OF CRIME

Where two or more people may be involved in a crime, the Crown may allege that they shared a common intention to commit the crime and to assist each other in doing so.

In such a case, where any one of the accused is alleged to have committed an offence in carrying out the shared purpose, then each of them who knew or ought to have known that the crime would be a probable consequence of carrying out the common purpose is also a party to the offence. All those convicted on the basis of common intention are subject to the same maximum penalty as the person who actually commits the crime.

c. JOINT POSSESSION

In cases of possession of drugs, stolen property, counterfeit money, or any other contraband, the prosecutor may allege that various people were jointly in possession of the items. The test in such cases is whether one person, with the knowledge and consent of the others, has the items in his or her custody or possession. If so, the items are deemed to be in the custody and possession of all of the accused.

The courts have added that there must be an element of control on the part of any one person accused in such cases. Many charges are dismissed on the basis that the accused had no control over the contraband matter. A classic illustration would be a situation in which one accused spent the night at the home of another accused, learning that the second accused had a narcotic on the premises, consenting to it being there, but not having any right to use it or remove it from the premises. In such a case, depending on all the circumstances, a judge may very well acquit the visitor.

d. ATTEMPTS

Anyone who tries to commit an offence is guilty of the attempt; it does not matter that it would have been impossible to commit the offence. The question is solely whether the person went beyond mere preparation to commit the offence. This will be a question of law to be determined in each case.

A person convicted of an attempt to commit an offence for which the maximum penalty is 14 years or less is punishable by a maximum term of one-half the longest term to which a person guilty of the offence would be liable.

In the case where the maximum penalty is imprisonment for life, a person guilty of the attempt would be liable to imprisonment for 14 years. For summary offences, the maximum penalty for the attempt is the same as for the actual offence, that is, six months.

e. COUNSELLING OR PROCURING

If you counsel or procure another person to be a party to an offence and that person is later a party to the offence, you can be charged with counselling or procuring. It doesn't matter if the offence is ultimately committed in a different way than you suggested.

If you are alleged to have counselled or procured, you are considered a party to every offence that the other person commits as a result of your counselling if you knew or ought to have known that an offence was likely to be committed.

If the offence is not committed, the maximum penalty for counselling or procuring or inciting another person to commit an indictable offence is the same as for a person who attempts to commit such offence.

If the offence is committed, the person who counsels, procures, or incites is subject to the same penalties as the person who actually commits the offence.

f. ACCESSORY AFTER THE FACT

An accessory after the fact is someone who knows that a person has been party to an offence and receives, comforts, or assists that person for the purpose of enabling him or her to escape. An accessory is subject to the same maximum penalties as a person who attempts to commit an offence. There is an exemption for a married person whose spouse has committed an offence. The law provides that no married person becomes an accessory by receiving, comforting, or assisting the other spouse for the purpose of enabling the other spouse to escape.

g. COMPOUNDING AN INDICTABLE OFFENCE

It is illegal to request or obtain or agree to obtain any valuable consideration, such as money, for yourself or any other person by agreeing to compound or conceal an indictable offence. You compound a felony when, having been directly injured by the felony, you agree with the criminal that you will not prosecute if the criminal makes reparation, or if you receive a reward or bribe not to prosecute.

This offence is not frequently charged any more, but is always available where a person who has been robbed takes his or her goods again, or takes other reward, as part of an agreement with the felon not to prosecute.

h. CONSPIRACY

A conspiracy is an agreement between two or more people to commit a criminal offence. The primary aspect of conspiracy charges is that the Crown is not required to prove that the offence was actually committed, or even that one step was taken toward its commission. All that is necessary is that the accused, or two or more of them, agreed among themselves to commit the offence. Police may have put the finger on them a moment after they agreed to commit the offence and before they have taken a further action. This makes no difference to the charge. If it is proved that they agreed, they can be convicted and subjected to the same maximum penalties as people who have actually committed the offence.

Conspiracy charges are a strong weapon in the prosecutor's arsenal; they frequently make co-defendants of persons who may barely know each other, or perhaps may not be acquainted at all.

8
SEARCH AND SEIZURE IN THE CRIMINAL CODE: GENERAL PROVISIONS

The general rule in the Criminal Code is that police have no right to search a place without a warrant. There are some exceptions to this rule dealt with in the following two chapters and in chapter 20 on weapons.

a. REQUIREMENT FOR A SEARCH WARRANT

Search warrants are issued only by justices of the peace, provincial court judges, or magistrates. To obtain a search warrant, an officer must swear a document informing the judge or justice of the peace that he or she believes on reasonable and probable grounds that a particular offence has been committed and believes that evidence can be found in a certain house, building, car, or other place. This evidence must be specified.

The warrant will authorize a person named in it or a peace officer to search a particular location or premises; it must set out the anticipated charge, the premises to be searched, and the evidence to be searched for. It should also set out the name of the owner or occupier of the premises. Moreover, the warrant will bear the date that it is issued by the justice of the peace.

b. YOUR RIGHTS WHEN PRESENTED WITH A SEARCH WARRANT

When the police arrive with a search warrant, you are entitled to see the warrant and demand a copy of it. In certain circumstances, you may wish to contact a lawyer and have someone from the lawyer's office come to monitor the search.

This is particularly desirable if there are many documents to be searched for in order to ensure that the warrant is complied with and that documents not authorized by the warrant are not seized. Police are obliged to carry the warrant with them and to produce it and allow you to examine it upon request.

The most important right that Canadians have in regard to searches is the right in Section 8 of the Charter of Rights and Freedoms. It provides that "everyone has the right to be secure against unreasonable search or seizure."

If you believe the search is illegal in the sense that the warrant was obtained without proper grounds, you should seek legal advice immediately. A search based on a search warrant obtained without proper grounds may be an infringement of your constitutional right to be secure against unreasonable search or seizure. Similarly, a search based on a warrant that is too vague or too broad in its terms may constitute an unreasonable search.

In these cases, you may be able to instruct a lawyer to bring an application in court to quash the search warrant. If the court grants such a motion, it will find that the search warrant was invalid, or that some part of it was invalid. Once the warrant is quashed, the court may direct the return of any items seized.

There are a number of questions that you should ask when studying the search warrant:

(a) Does it set out a criminal offence?

(b) Does it correctly identify the place to be searched? (If the address on the warrant is not your address, you should tell the police so, as they then have no right to enter.)

(c) If the warrant is directed to the premises of a specific person it may be invalid for you if it specifically names someone else as occupant. You may be able to refuse entry in these circumstances, and you should contact a lawyer immediately.

(d) Is the document vague in setting out the materials to be searched for? Is it too broad in authorizing police to take any sort of documents from the premises? In either of these cases, the warrant may be subject to being quashed.

(e) What is the date on the search warrant? Warrants are valid on the day specified and for a reasonable time thereafter. If the search is being made after the date on which the warrant was obtained, you should consult legal counsel as it may be that the validity can be challenged on this basis.

(f) Ascertain that the officer to whom the warrant is directed is present.

(g) If the search is at night, does the warrant authorize this? Search warrants normally must be executed by day, between 6:00 a.m. and 9:00 p.m. unless there is specific provision for execution by night.

(h) Watch for any other matters which strike you as irregular and on which you wish to seek legal advice.

Search warrants under the Criminal Code permit an officer to search a place, house, premises, apartment, or car. They do not allow an officer to search a person. If an officer tries to search you, you may ask if you are under arrest. If you are told that you are not, you may refuse to be searched. There is no general power to search an individual who is not under arrest.

Any statement made by you or any other person on the premises to a police officer during the course of a search may be used later in court against you or that person if charges are laid. It is important to observe the activities of the police during the search, but not to make any comments.

When police complete the search, which you must permit them to do if the warrant is correctly issued, they must take anything that they have seized to the person who issued the warrant. They must also file a written report stating what was found and what occurred during the search.

c. **SEARCH OF MOTOR VEHICLE**

In general, when police search a motor vehicle, they are in exactly the same position as they are when searching houses or apartments. A motor vehicle is a private place. Police must go before a justice of the peace or a provincial court judge or magistrate and swear an information specifying the motor vehicle to be searched and the offence for which evidence is being sought. They must swear that they have reasonable and probable grounds to believe that a particular offence has been committed or is being committed by using the vehicle or in the vehicle or that evidence can be found in the vehicle.

However, arbitrary searches of vehicles are sometimes carried out under the cloak of the search provisions of the narcotics and other drugs laws, liquor laws, customs, and weapons laws.

The searches under these statutory provisions may be found by the courts to violate Section 8 of the Constitution unless they are based on reasonable grounds.

d. TELEWARRANTS

An amendment to the Criminal Code has resulted in the creation of the telewarrant, a form of search authorization obtained by a police officer via a telephone call or other telecommunication, such as a facsimile (FAX) transmission, to a judicial officer.

Just as with regular search warrants, a police officer must have reasonable and probable grounds for a search, and the circumstances must be such that it is impracticable to obtain an ordinary search warrant, such as where there is a likelihood that evidence would be destroyed in the time it would take to appear before a justice of the peace.

To obtain a telewarrant, a police officer must phone the justice of the peace and provide the usual details of persons and premises to be searched, offences for which evidence is being sought, and grounds for the search. In addition, the police officer must satisfy the justice of the peace that it would be impracticable to obtain a warrant in the usual manner. The telephone call or other form of telecommunication is recorded and a transcript made. This written version of the oral authorization must be taken to the premises to be searched and made available for inspection by the person whose premises are being searched.

e. REMEDIES FOR ILLEGAL SEARCH OR SEIZURE

One of the rights that a person has when a search is unreasonable is to apply to a court to quash the unreasonable search and to order the return of the goods seized.

When criminal charges are laid as a result of evidence found during an unreasonable search, an application can be made under Section 24(2) of the Charter to exclude the evidence from the trial on the basis that it was obtained by infringement of Charter rights, and that to receive it in evidence would bring the administration of justice into disrepute.

In addition, Section 24(1) of the Charter provides that anyone whose rights have been infringed or denied may apply to a court to obtain "such remedy as the court considers appropriate and just" in the circumstances. Where a constitutional right has been disregarded, a court has jurisdiction under Section 24(1) to fashion a remedy that is "appropriate and just." This may consist of quashing the charges against the accused, or staying or stopping the proceedings, or dismissing the charge. It may also include awarding damages for illegal search and seizure. The range of remedies that are available under the Charter will not be determined until after the courts have ruled on a number of cases.

f. REVIEW OF BASIS FOR ISSUING SEARCH WARRANT

Once a search warrant has been executed, and items seized in the search have been brought before a justice of the peace, the Supreme Court of Canada has held that any member of the public is entitled to inspect the search warrant and the information on which it was based unless such disclosure would subvert the ends of justice, or unless the judicial documents might be used for an improper purpose.

Parliament has introduced legislation to prohibit the press or other media from publishing the identity of the person whose premises have been searched or the location of the search, unless a charge results and the accused appears in court or consents to publication. However, several lower court decisions have held that this is an unconstitutional restriction on freedom of the press. The matter has yet to go to the Supreme Court of Canada.

g. SOLICITOR AND CLIENT PRIVILEGE

Amendments have also been incorporated into the Criminal Code that establish special procedures to ensure that privileged communications between lawyer and client are kept confidential where documents have been seized.

Police officers who seize documents for which solicitor/client privilege is claimed are required to place such documents in a sealed envelope, which is then given to a sheriff or court officer for safe keeping.

If a document is seized and placed in the custody of the sheriff or court officer, the prosecutor, the client, or the lawyer may, within 14 days from the day the document was placed in custody, apply to a judge for an order appointing a place and a day to determine the question of whether the document should be disclosed. The judge has the discretion to inspect the documents and allow the prosecutor to inspect the documents to determine whether they ought to be disclosed. If the judge makes the determination that the documents fall within solicitor/client privilege, then they are not liable to be seized and must be returned to the lawyer's office.

9

SEARCH AND SEIZURE IN THE CRIMINAL CODE: SPECIAL PROVISIONS RELATING TO GAMBLING, BETTING, OBSCENITY, AND PROSTITUTION CASES

Wider powers of search are available to police officers investigating premises allegedly used for gambling, betting, distribution of obscene literature, or prostitution. There are specific extraordinary powers under the Criminal Code that authorize expedient searches of such premises.

a. GAMBLING AND BETTING

The gambling and betting businesses are kept under a tight control by the government, which authorizes operations such as pari-mutuel betting through race tracks. The major lottery games are the national and provincial lotteries which only the federal and provincial governments are permitted to conduct. Provincial governments are also empowered to license charitable or religious organizations as well as agricultural fairs to conduct certain kinds of lotteries, and any person to operate a place of amusement with games under a specific licence.

Private bets by people not engaged in the business of betting are lawful. Any person or association may also serve as custodian of monies to be paid to the winner of a lawful race, sport, or game, or to the winner of a bet among not more than 10 individuals.

The pari-mutuel betting at race tracks is authorized and controlled by the Minister of Agriculture.

Such things as off-track betting establishments, publicly available gaming, and gambling houses are absolutely illegal under the Criminal Code. There is a narrow range of permission for legal gaming available to incorporated *bona fide* social clubs or their branches, provided that the keeper of the game does not take a cut from the bets or any fee from the players. However, if illegal gambling occurs on the premises, not only is the keeper of the premises liable to conviction, but also anybody found there and the landlord, owner, or occupier of the premises.

b. SEARCH OF GAMBLING AND BETTING HOUSES

The Criminal Code refers to gambling and betting houses, as well as bawdy (prostitution) houses, as disorderly houses. A police officer who believes illegal gaming, gambling, lotteries, or betting is occurring in a particular premises must give a report in writing to a justice of the peace showing that he or she has reasonable grounds for this belief. The justice can issue a warrant empowering the police officer to enter and search the place by day or night and seize anything that may be evidence of such offence.

Any act to prevent, delay, or obstruct the officer in the execution of this search warrant may be a summary offence. Evidence at trial that a police officer was wilfully prevented, obstructed, or delayed in entering the premises may be treated as proof that the house is a disorderly house.

c. SEARCH OF GAMING HOUSE WITHOUT WARRANT

There is also provision for search of a common gaming house without a warrant where a police officer finds people using the premises as a common gaming house.

The Criminal Code defines game as a "game of chance or mixed skill and chance." A common gaming house is a place kept for gain to which people go for the purpose of playing games; or a place in which one of the players, but not all of the players, keeps a bank; or where a portion of the bets or proceeds is paid to the keeper of the place; or where the keeper takes a fee from players for the privilege of playing;

or where the chances of winning are not equally favorable to all persons who play.

d. ARREST AND QUESTIONING OF FOUND-INS

If you are found in a common gaming or betting house, you are liable to arrest and may be charged with a summary offence. You have the right to counsel and would do well to assert this right.

The Criminal Code provides that anyone apprehended during a search by warrant can be taken before the magistrate or justice for questioning about the purposes of the premises in which they were found and any matter that occurred during the search. Anyone who refuses to answer may be kept in custody for up to eight days, the same as a witness who refuses to answer questions in a trial. However, any answers given cannot be used as evidence against the found-in except in a perjury case.

e. SEARCH OF A COMMON BAWDY HOUSE

The Criminal Code defines a common bawdy house as a place kept or occupied or resorted to by one or more persons for the purpose of prostitution or for the practice of indecent acts.

A search warrant will be granted by a justice when a police officer files a written report stating that he or she has reasonable grounds to believe that the offence of keeping a common bawdy house is being committed at a given premises.

The warrant empowers the police officer to seize evidence, arrest anybody found inside, and arrest the keeper of the place.

Obstruction of the officer attempting to enter and search is itself a criminal office and may lead to a presumption during trial that the place was a disorderly house.

A special search warrant is available in cases where it is alleged that a female person has been enticed to or concealed in a common bawdy house. In such cases, a justice of the peace may issue a warrant if satisfied on the basis of a sworn information from a police officer that there is reasonable ground to believe such a female may be found on the premises.

The warrant can require the woman and the keeper of the premises to be brought before the justice. This warrant also allows police to use force to enter.

f. FOUND-INS IN A BAWDY HOUSE

The people found in a house of prostitution during a search by warrant can be brought before a justice of the peace and questioned about the purpose for which the place was used and any occurrence during the search.

You must answer these questions, although you would be entitled to invoke your right to consult a lawyer before answering questions.

If the keeper of a common bawdy house is convicted, this conviction will be treated as proof that the premises were a disorderly house as alleged in the trials of those people found in the house.

Taxi drivers and other people who are regularly asked where the "best houses" are found should bear in mind the provisions of Section 194 of the Criminal Code. This section makes it a criminal offence punishable on summary conviction ($2 000 fine or six months in jail, or both) to knowingly take, transport, direct, or offer to take anyone to a common bawdy house.

g. OBSCENITY CASES

Police can seize copies of any allegedly obscene publications being kept for sale or distribution at news and magazine stores.

Police must have a search warrant issued by a judge authorizing the seizure. To obtain the warrant, a police officer must swear on oath that there are reasonable grounds for believing that the publication is obscene. According to the Criminal Code, a publication is obscene if "a dominant characteristic...is the undue exploitation of sex, or of sex and any one or more of the following subjects, namely, crime, horror, cruelty, and violence...."

It is not necessary that charges be laid against the owner, but within seven days the owner shall be summonsed to appear and show cause why the matter seized should not be forfeited to the Crown. If you are the owner or occupier, you are entitled to appear with counsel, ask questions, call evidence of community standards, and so on.

The court will return the books or materials to the person from whom they were seized if it is not satisfied that the publications are obscene and if the Crown has not appealed against that finding.

You may challenge the search warrant on the grounds that the terms of the warrant are too wide, that it is unnecessary to seize every copy of the publication (if there are many), that other documents (such as bookkeeping records of the firm) were wrongfully seized, that there is no reasonable basis for believing the material seized is obscene, or any of the other grounds for attacking the validity of a warrant.

In addition, there is an appeal against the finding of a judge that a publication is obscene.

10
SEARCH AND SEIZURE UNDER THE INCOME TAX LAWS

The following sections deal only with powers of search and seizure in an investigation under the Income Tax Act where Revenue Canada appears to be looking for evidence to support criminal charges.

Some of the information on the powers of auditors under the Income Tax Act is applicable to cases where it will ultimately be alleged that you as a taxpayer have arranged your affairs in such manner that you have paid less tax than the tax department believes you should pay, but that no criminal offence has been committed. This is the usual case.

a. OFFENCES UNDER THE INCOME TAX ACT

There are many criminal offences under the Income Tax Act, too numerous to mention here. Tax evasion is the most serious offence. It includes making deceptive statements in a tax return, destroying, altering, secreting, or otherwise disposing of books or records to evade payment of a tax imposed by the act, or conspiring to do any of these things. Failing to file tax returns is also an offence.

Offences of tax evasion may be proceeded with by summary conviction offence or by indictment. Where summary proceedings are taken (meaning the taxpayer will not have a preliminary hearing or a right to a jury trial), the maximum penalties are a fine of not less than 25% and not more than double the amount of tax sought to be evaded, or both a fine and imprisonment of up to two years.

Where the indictable proceedings are taken, the maximum penalty is five years in prison and the minimum, two months in prison.

b. GENERAL POWERS OF AUDITORS

Auditors and investigators acting under the income tax laws have extremely broad powers to enter premises and examine records and documents and to seize them if satisfied that there may be an offence under the Income Tax Act.

The following basic rules apply in the course of a Revenue Canada investigation:

(a) Auditors may at all reasonable times enter into business premises to audit or examine the books and records and any accounts, vouchers, letters, telegrams, or other documents relating to the amount of tax payable.

(b) They may require the owner or manager of the property or business to assist them with the audit or examination and to answer proper questions relating to the audit or examination orally or in writing, on oath or by statutory declaration. You may have your lawyer or accountant present. Where business is carried on at a dwelling house, an authorized person may not enter that dwelling house without the consent of the occupant, except with a search warrant.

Note that the judge who hears an application by Revenue Canada for a warrant has the discretion to refuse the warrant but may instead order the occupant of the dwelling house to provide reasonable access to the document or property in question, or make any other order which would be appropriate in the circumstances.

c. POWER OF AN AUDITOR TO SEIZE DOCUMENTS

Auditors no longer have the authority to seize any documents, books, records, papers, or things uncovered during the course of an audit that might be required as evidence as to the violation of any provision under the act or regulations.

These former powers of auditors, which also allowed Revenue Canada to retain any documents for 120 days unless further ordered by a court, were successfully challenged on the basis that the right in Section 8 of the Charter to be free from unreasonable search or seizure was violated. Documents may now be seized only by warrant.

d. DEMAND LETTER FOR INFORMATION

The tax laws permit the minister responsible for Revenue Canada to send a registered letter of demand to a taxpayer requesting information or a supplemental return, or production of any books, letters, accounts, invoices, statements, or other documents.

e. SEARCH WARRANTS UNDER THE INCOME TAX ACT

To obtain a search warrant under the Income Tax Act, the minister responsible for Revenue Canada must have the approval of a judge of the superior or county court. Once such approval has been granted, the minister can authorize in writing any member of the department, together with members of the RCMP or other police officers, to search, by force if necessary, any specified building, receptacle, or place for documents, books, records, papers, or things that could provide evidence of a violation of the Income Tax Act or the Regulations. These things may be seized and kept until they are produced in court proceedings, unless they are not required for an investigation or criminal proceeding, or not seized in accordance with the warrant or the act.

The application to a county or superior court judge must be supported by sworn evidence, setting out that the minister has reasonable and probable grounds to believe that a violation of the act has been committed or is likely to be committed, that a document that may afford evidence of the commission of the offence is likely to be found, and that the building, place, or receptacle specified is likely to contain such a document or thing.

Once again, this is an application that the minister is entitled to make on an *ex parte* basis, which means the taxpayer is not entitled to be represented. However, the ex parte feature of this procedure is not unusual; search warrants under the Criminal Code are always granted in ex parte proceedings before a justice of the peace or a judge.

f. SEIZURE OF DOCUMENTS FROM A LAWYER'S OFFICE

It is a general rule of law that when you are in a superior court you are entitled to refuse to disclose what you have told your lawyer on grounds of professional confidence. This is referred to as solicitor/client privilege and the usual rule is that you are not compelled to disclose any communication passing between you and your lawyer unless such communication is not protected as in the case where it was in furtherance of a crime.

The law provides for sealing of documents about to be seized from a lawyer when there is a question of privilege. The package must be placed in the custody of the sheriff of the district or county in which the seizure was made or in the custody of some other person whom the Revenue Canada officer and the lawyer agree should act as custodian.

The lawyer or client is then entitled to apply within fourteen days, giving three days notice to the Deputy Attorney General of Canada, for an order setting a day to decide the question of whether the solicitor/client privilege applies to the document.

Such an application is heard in the judge's chambers. The judge is entitled to inspect the document, although he or she must ensure that it is re-packaged and re-sealed. If the judge agrees that the solicitor/client privilege applies to the document, the custodian will be ordered to return the document to the lawyer.

If the judge believes the privilege does not apply, he or she can order that it be delivered to someone designated by the deputy minister responsible for Revenue Canada — Taxation.

g. EXAMINATION OF BANK DOCUMENTS

Many people erroneously believe that Revenue Canada auditors are not entitled to examine documents relating to bank transactions that are in the possession of their banker. The fact is that bank transactions are often a very important aspect of the auditor's investigation and the act empowers the auditor to ask for a written authorization to examine accounts at a bank. In these circumstances, the banker has no choice and the documents must be provided for examination.

It seems clear that no search of a safety deposit box could be made without a written search authorization. It is arguable that a safety deposit box search authorization must be directed to the person who leases the box, not to the bank. It is in a sense property that is in control of the taxpayer at the time, and not property that is in control of the bank.

h. STATEMENTS MADE TO AUDITORS OR INVESTIGATORS

Any statement you make to a Revenue Canada auditor or investigator can be used against you if you are later charged with a criminal offence under the Income Tax Act.

The act does not deal with the right against self-incrimination, but makes it a requirement to answer "proper questions" during the course of an audit or examination. It may be quite important to consult with a lawyer or accountant before answering such questions. You might build a case against yourself by answering the same question in two different ways during two different visits by the auditor. This is something that could happen as a result of mere carelessness, rather than any real intention to mislead the auditor.

i. THE COMPLIANCE RULE

The Income Tax Act requires you to do everything you are required to do in the course of searches and investigations under the act. In particular, it is an offence to hinder or molest or interfere with any auditor or investigator of Revenue Canada who is doing anything that is authorized or to prevent or attempt to prevent any person from doing such things.

Violation of this section of the Income Tax Act is a summary offence and upon conviction a person is liable to a fine of from $200 to $10 000, or a fine and imprisonment for up to six months.

11
THE NARCOTICS LAWS

Illegal possession and distribution of drugs are two of the crimes most commonly committed in North America. The drug laws, like earlier laws prohibiting alcohol, are virtually impossible to enforce. The number of people arrested under existing drug laws is minimal in comparison with the numbers who choose to defy the law and use illegal drugs.

In Canada, drugs are banned primarily under two statutes: the Narcotic Control Act and the Food and Drugs Act.

The Narcotic Control Act bans the use of cannabis marijuana, cannabis resin (hashish), cannabinol, pyrohexyl, and tetrahydrocannabinol (THC). It also bans opium, codeine, morphine, diacetylmorphine (heroin), and cocaine.

Marijuana consists of the flowering tops, leaves, seeds, and stems of the hemp plant. It grows easily throughout North America and in most other countries of the world.

Hashish is the pure resin of the marijuana plant and is available in solid or liquid form. THC, or tetrahydrocannabinol, is the active ingredient of marijuana. It can be synthesized and comes in capsule, powder, or liquid form. There is very little pure THC available.

Opium is derived from the dried juices of the seeds of the opium poppy. Morphine and codeine are derivatives of opium, and heroin is a derivative of morphine.

Cocaine is a derivative of the South American coca plant. The raw processing occurs in "factories" in Bolivia, Peru, and Columbia, and the drug reaches North America in a whitish, powder form.

a. POSSESSION

In Canada it is *not* legal to possess even a small amount of a narcotic for personal use. Possession of any of these drugs, other than under licence or prescription for medicinal purposes, is an offence under the Narcotic Control Act.

The prosecutor may proceed against you summarily or by indictment. If you are brought before the court, the prosecutor will choose to proceed by summary offence where, for example, a small amount of narcotics is involved and it is your first offence. The maximum penalties for a first conviction on a summary offence are a fine of $1 000, imprisonment for six months or both. The maximum penalties for a subsequent conviction upon summary procedure are a fine of $2 000 or imprisonment for one year or both.

In most parts of Canada, if you are convicted of possession of a small amount of marijuana and it is your first offence, you will probably receive a fine or be put on probation. In some circumstances, you may also receive absolute or conditional discharge (see chapter 30). If you are convicted of a second offence, the penalty will be stiffer, and could be a short jail term.

b. CULTIVATION

It is illegal to cultivate opium poppy or marijuana except under a research licence granted by the federal government. There is no right under Canadian law as it presently stands to grow even a few marijuana plants for your own use. Unlawful cultivation of *any* marijuana plants is an indictable offence carrying a maximum penalty of seven years in jail.

The Narcotic Control Act gives the Minister of Health and Welfare Canada the power to order the destruction of any growing plant of opium poppy or marijuana that has not been cultivated under a lawfully issued licence.

c. TRAFFICKING

Trafficking in a narcotic is an indictable offence and carries a maximum penalty of life imprisonment. The definition of trafficking is very wide. It includes manufacturing, selling, giving, administering, transporting, sending, delivering, or distributing. It also includes offering to do any of these things.

If you are arrested and charged with trafficking, it is probable that you will be alleged to have sold the drugs to an undercover agent. In these circumstances, you should say nothing other than to demand the right to telephone your lawyer.

The most frequent trafficking charges are made when the accused has sold some drugs to an undercover police officer.

Trafficking, even in so-called "soft drugs," is treated very seriously by the courts.

d. POSSESSION FOR THE PURPOSE OF TRAFFICKING

The law does not state what amount of narcotics will take you from a charge of mere possession to a charge of possession for the purpose of trafficking.

The decision whether to lay a charge of simple possession or possession for the purpose of trafficking depends on the circumstances of the case. The police have some discretion: If the police find the paraphernalia of trafficking, such as weigh scales, packaging materials, large amounts of money, or lists of names with amount of drugs and money, the charge is more likely to be possession for the purpose of trafficking.

Historically, the law has been stacked against an accused charged with possession for the purpose of trafficking because the presumption of innocence did not apply. Once the court found the accused was in possession of the narcotic or other drug, he or she was presumed to be guilty of possession for the purpose of trafficking. The onus was on the accused to prove that possession was not for the purpose of trafficking.

These laws were successfully challenged on the basis that they violated the presumption of innocence which became a constitutional right on April 17, 1982 when it was included in the Charter of Rights and Freedoms.

In cases of trafficking or possession for the purpose of trafficking, it is not necessarily a defence that the drug, when analyzed, proves to be a different drug than the one the accused was claimed to be selling. For example, a person may have a drug he or she believes is heroin. If it is sold to an undercover officer and analyzed to be cocaine, the prosecutor can charge the accused with trafficking a drug "held to be" heroin, and the court can convict the accused of that offence.

e. IMPORTING

Importing a narcotic into Canada is the most severe charge under the Narcotic Control Act. A conviction for importing or for exporting (which is very uncommon), used to carry a minimum penalty of seven years in jail. However, the Supreme Court of Canada held the minimum penalty to be unconstitutional on the basis that it constituted cruel and unusual punishment. This determination was made because the penalty section led to the imposition of totally disproportionate terms of imprisonment in certain circumstances. For example, a person crossing the border with a small amount of marijuana for personal use was subject to the same seven year jail term as an importer of several pounds of marijuana for resale purposes.

While there is no longer a minimum penalty, the maximum sentence remains life imprisonment.

12
THE FOOD AND DRUGS ACT

a. RESTRICTED DRUGS

Many of the common hallucinogenic drugs are restricted under Schedule H of the Food and Drugs Act. These include, LSD, MDA, DMT, DET, MMDA, LBJ, and psilocybin. New drugs are added to the list from time to time. It is unlawful to possess, to possess for the purpose of trafficking, or to traffic in these drugs.

b. PENALTIES FOR POSSESSION OF RESTRICTED DRUGS

Should you be charged with illegal possession of any restricted drug such as LSD or MDA, the prosecutor may proceed against you by either summary or indictable offence rules, just as for possession of narcotics.

If the prosecutor chooses to proceed against you summarily, the maximum penalties for a first offence are a fine of $1 000, or imprisonment for six months, or both. For a subsequent offence, the penalties are again the same as possession of marijuana — a maximum fine of $2 000, or imprisonment for 12 months, or both.

If you are charged with an indictable offence, the maximum penalties are a fine of $5 000, or imprisonment for three years, or both. The penalties are lighter than for an indictable offence of possession under the Narcotic Control Act. However, most judges will impose much the same sentence for possession of LSD as for possession of marijuana.

c. TRAFFICKING IN RESTRICTED DRUGS

Trafficking under the Food and Drugs Act includes manufacturing, delivering, exporting, importing, transporting, or selling. Note that this definition is substantially different from the definition of trafficking in the Narcotic Control Act. Under the latter act, importing is a separate offence, carrying harsher penalties than for trafficking. Also, the act of "giving" is not specified as a method of unlawful trafficking in the Food and Drugs Act.

Maximum penalties for trafficking under the Food and Drugs Act are less severe than those provided in the Narcotic Control Act. The prosecutor has the option of proceeding by summary or indictable offence.

If the prosecutor proceeds summarily, the maximum penalty is 18 months in prison; by indictment, the maximum is 10 years. The same rules apply to offences of possession for the purpose of trafficking. Under the Narcotic Control Act, the maximum penalty for these offences is always life imprisonment. Federal prosecutors invariably proceed by indictment in cases of trafficking and possession for the purposes of trafficking under the Food and Drugs Act.

It is also an offence to traffic in a substance "held out" or represented to be a restricted drug.

d. CONTROLLED DRUGS

Two fairly commonly known groups of drugs are "controlled drugs" under Schedule G of the Food and Drugs Act. The amphetamine group includes those drugs often called "uppers:" methamphetamine, benzphetamine, and such products as dexedrine, benzedrine, methedrine, and dexamyl. The second group is the barbiturates, commonly known as "downers" as they are depressants used medically as sleeping pills and tranquilizers.

e. POSSESSION OF CONTROLLED DRUGS NOT AN OFFENCE

It is not an offence under the Food and Drugs Act simply to be in possession of amphetamines or barbiturates for personal use. However, normally these drugs can be obtained for personal use only through a valid prescription authorized by a licensed physician. It is an offence to obtain these drugs by means of a false prescription or any other false pretense.

It is also an offence under the Food and Drugs Act to possess amphetamines or barbiturates for the purpose of trafficking in them.

f. TRAFFICKING IN CONTROLLED DRUGS

Federal prosecutors have the option of proceeding against a person on a charge of trafficking or possession for the purpose of trafficking in a controlled drug by summary conviction proceedings or by indictment. The invariable rule is that these cases are prosecuted by indictment, bringing the heavier penalties into play upon conviction. The maximum penalties for trafficking in controlled drugs are the same as for trafficking in restricted drugs: 18 months and 10 years respectively, depending on whether the proceedings are summary or indictable. It is also an offence to traffic in a substance held out to be a controlled drug.

13
THE DRUG LAWS — SEARCH AND SEIZURE

Under the Narcotic Control Act, the police have wide powers to search for illegal drugs. They can search, without a warrant, any place that is not a residence or appended to a residence. They can also search any person found in such a place.

To do these things, however, the police officers must first have a reasonable belief that they will find illegal drugs. The law provides no criteria for determining what a "reasonable belief" may be.

However, the Charter of Rights and Freedoms in Section 8 provides that everyone has the right to be secure against unreasonable search or seizure. The courts will work out on a case-by-case basis the rules that must be applied.

There are many issues to be resolved. The law, as it stands, can be interpreted very loosely. The word place is not defined. It isn't restricted in any way, except that it does not apply to a dwelling. Theoretically it could apply to a car or any other vehicle, or any building that is not a residence. It could mean any place (e.g., a public plaza, a shopping centre, a street, a park, a department store, or a parking lot).

The first cases under the Charter seem to indicate that if a search is made without reasonable grounds, for example, on mere conjecture or suspicion, anything found as a result of the search may be rejected as evidence. The test is whether the use of such illegally obtained evidence will bring the administration of justice into disrepute. This is discussed in more detail in chapter 34.

a. SEARCH OF PERSON

Police officers seeking to search a person without a warrant under the narcotics laws must tell the suspect under what law they are making the search.

The search must be based on a reasonable belief that drugs will be found. A person who believes that his or her rights are being abused may object to the search. Make it clear that it is being done without your consent in order to preserve your remedies for unlawful search and seizure.

If anything is seized, and you are questioned about it, it is advisable to consult with a lawyer before making any statements. Possession is a technical matter in law, and a casual or careless statement may be misconstrued. You also may incriminate yourself by making statements.

b. SEARCH OF VEHICLE

If your car is stopped by a police officer who asks you to get out so that he or she can search, you may object and ask to see a search warrant. If the officer does not have one but is planning to search under either the Narcotic Control Act, or the Food and Drugs Act, then you can ask on what grounds. If the officer persists, let the search go ahead. You are not required to answer questions about who owns anything that is in the vehicle.

The Narcotic Control Act authorizes police to seize a conveyance, such as a motor car, in which a narcotic is found. When this happens, and a person is convicted of an offence of trafficking, possession for the purpose of trafficking, importing, or exporting a narcotic, the court can order that the vehicle used for the offence be forfeited to the state. The owner of the vehicle, however, can appeal against this order.

c. ILLEGAL SEARCHES

If the police are not making a search under the Narcotic Control Act or under another law that must be stated, then the search may be illegal and unconstitutional as being unreasonable search and seizure.

You may, in these circumstances, defend your property using only as much force as is reasonably necessary to prevent the illegal search or seizure. However, it is usually wiser only to object to the illegal search, making it clear that you do not consent to it, with a view to taking legal remedies later.

d. SEARCH OF RESIDENCE

Police officers have no right to search a residence for illegal drugs unless they have a search warrant or a telewarrant. A mobile home or a tent is your residence if you happen to live there. The police must have a *reasonable belief* that there is an illegal drug on your premises before searching.

While a search is proceeding, you may wish to keep an observant eye on the activities of the officers involved. Your recollection of events may be important later in court.

Both the Narcotic Control Act and the Food and Drugs Act authorize police to break doors, windows, locks, fasteners, floors, walls, ceilings, compartments, plumbing fixtures, boxes, containers, or anything else they consider to be necessary to their search. If the search is illegal, you may sue for recovery of the damage and possibly lay mischief charges against the officers.

A court may also award other remedies considered to be "appropriate and just in the circumstances" according to Section 24(1) of the Charter of Rights and Freedoms.

Among the things that a court might do is direct the police to return items seized from you. The court could also dismiss charges laid against you based on material seized during an unlawful search.

e. TELEWARRANTS

Telewarrants, search warrants obtained orally by a telephone submission to a justice of the peace, have been discussed in other chapters. They are extensively used in narcotic and other drug investigations, in the same way that writs of assistance were once used in these cases.

14
DRUG TRIALS — WHAT THE PROSECUTOR MUST PROVE

When you are charged with possession of marijuana, the first chore of the prosecutor is to prove the drug itself. A chemist must be engaged to prove that the substance you had was, in fact, marijuana.

A certificate of analysis may be served on you a reasonable time before trial. This certificate will enable the prosecutor to prove the drug without calling in the analyst to give evidence.

As long as there is enough of the drug to analyze, no matter how small the amount, you may be charged and convicted. Police sometimes arrest known addicts and seize spoons or hypodermic kits containing a minuscule amount of heroin.

Soft drug searches may be brought on the basis of a residue of cannabis resin on a pipe or other smoking paraphernalia. This residue is sufficient for analysis. A few seeds or stems will support a charge of possession.

If you haven't confessed to the offence, or pleaded guilty, the prosecutor is obliged to prove all the following points:

(a) That you had knowledge that the substance was an illegal drug

(b) That you knowingly had the drug in your possession (either on your personal possession or in some other place)

(c) That your possession was voluntary (you consented to it)

(d) That you had some measure of control over the drug and its whereabouts

These are the essential elements of illegal possession. If proof of any one of them is lacking, you will be acquitted.

The same rules do not apply to trafficking cases. If you are accused in such a case, you may be found guilty even if you did not know which particular drug you were selling. For example, in one recent case decided by the Supreme Court of Canada, the accused sold what he thought was MDA to a police officer. It turned out to be LSD. The accused was convicted of trafficking LSD, even though he believed he had MDA.

a. WHY RETAIN A LAWYER?

Even simple possession cases are criminal charges in Canada and conviction can result. Proof of possession is a technical matter in law and often a trained lawyer will appreciate distinctions and defences that will not be readily apparent to a lay person. It is always a good idea to speak to a lawyer before pleading to a drug charge.

b. INCRIMINATING EVIDENCE

Statements made to police and exhibits seized from your possession may assist the police in proving their case. For example, such items as resin-stained pipes or "roach" clips or cigarette papers may help to prove a possession of cannabis charge; possession of a large amount of cash, packages of small plastic bags, and kitchen scales may be used as evidence in a possession for trafficking case.

Special paraphernalia linked to the use of or traffic in a particular drug may always afford evidence for the police. Needle or "track" marks on the arms of a suspected heroin user may provide incriminating evidence.

c. SHOULD THE ACCUSED TESTIFY?

A real difficulty in many drug possession cases is to decide whether the accused should testify on his or her own behalf. Many of these cases are proved by circumstantial evidence. If the accused person testifies, there is always the danger that the judge may not believe the testimony and may make a conviction, which wouldn't have happened if there had been no defence evidence. A thin line sometimes divides cases where it is necessary for the accused to testify and cases where the accused can be acquitted without testimony.

d. INVOLUNTARY POSSESSION

The issue of voluntariness may also arise. Suppose somebody mails you a pound of hashish you did not know about or want. The narcotics officers burst in two minutes after the mail carrier has left. You are holding the wrapper with your name and address on it, and the opened package of hashish is sitting on the table because you haven't yet decided how to get rid of it.

The prosecutor will have trouble establishing that you were expecting the package or that you intended to keep it. You would testify that you were an involuntary possessor. For an acquittal, the judge must believe your evidence, or at least have doubt as to your guilt.

Where both elements of knowledge are proved and there is some evidence of voluntariness, there may be a defence based upon control. Suppose that you are visiting friends, and there is some marijuana on the kitchen table. You are the only person sitting at the table when narcotics officers arrive, but you are a visitor and have no right to the drug and no control over its use.

In this case, the owner of the drug may take the protection against self-incrimination offered by the Canada Evidence Act and give evidence at your trial. Section 5 of the Canada Evidence Act allows him or her to refuse to answer incriminating questions until the judge grants protection.

A person testifying under the Canada Evidence Act must ask for the protection of that act for each question that may require an incriminating answer. In these circumstances, you probably won't be convicted. You are not in possession unless the prosecutor proves that you had a measure of control over the drug.

In addition, Section 13 of the Charter of Rights and Freedoms now provides that a witness who testifies in any case has the right "not to have any incriminating evidence so given used to incriminate that witness in any other proceedings." There is obviously an exception in the case of a prosecution for perjury, or lying in court under oath.

15
DRINKING AND DRIVING LAWS

There are few crimes that have been so frequently contemplated or committed by Canadians as those of impaired driving, driving with more than 80 milligrams of alcohol per 100 millilitres of blood (referred to as over .08 driving.), and refusing to provide breath samples. Indeed, these are the most common crimes in our country.

A multitude of persons, who would never consider themselves to be or be considered by others to be criminal in any usual sense of the word, are charged with alcohol-related driving offences. Yet these are serious charges in our Criminal Code. They may result in a criminal record, as well as having serious consequences, such as suspension of the driver's licence, upon conviction.

The following is not intended to be an exhaustive review of the subject, but is a general outline of the legal procedures and the rights of suspects under these laws.

a. **WHAT ARE THE DRINKING AND DRIVING OFFENCES?**

There are three distinct offences and in a given case at least two of them may be charged:

  (a) Driving or being in care or control of a motor vehicle while your ability to drive is impaired by alcohol or a drug (Very rarely are drug users charged, as proof is difficult without a full confession that a drug was taken.)

  (b) Driving or being in care or control of a motor vehicle with more than .08 alcohol to blood ratio

(c) Refusing without reasonable excuse to provide samples of breath for analysis to determine the proportion of alcohol in the blood after a proper demand for such samples

The minimum and maximum penalties for each of the three offences is the same. For a first offence, there is a minimum $300 fine and maximum $2 000 fine, or up to six months in jail, or both. The usual penalty for a first offence is a fine.

For a second offence, the minimum penalty is two weeks in jail if the prosecutor requests the statutory minimum; the maximum penalty is six months in jail. If a jail term is imposed there will normally be no fine. This applies where the Crown has proceeded by way of summary conviction. Where the Crown has proceeded by way of indictment, the maximum penalty is five years in jail.

For a third offence, the minimum penalty is 90 days in jail if the prosecutor has proved the required notice for a statutory third offence. The maximum penalty is six months in jail and, again, if a jail term is imposed there will normally be no fine. If the Crown proceeds by way of indictment, the maximum penalty is five years.

Parliament has also introduced the new offence of impaired driving causing bodily harm. Anyone found guilty of this indictable offence may be imprisoned for up to 10 years. Another new offence is that of impaired driving causing death, which is also an indictable offence. The maximum term of imprisonment for this offence is 14 years.

It is important to remember that a prosecutor is entitled to request the statutory minimum jail terms for second and third offences. If the prosecutor has laid the ground work and you are convicted of a second or third offence, a judge has no discretion in the matter of whether to impose a jail term. He or she must impose a jail term and, as above, on the third offence the jail term must be at least three months.

The Criminal Code now provides for a mandatory order of prohibition from driving where a person has been convicted of impaired driving or driving with a blood alcohol level over .08. For a first offence, the mandatory order of prohibition must be for not less than three months and not more than three years; for a second offence, not less than six months and not greater than three years; and for each subsequent offence, a period of not less than one year and no more than three years.

However, where a person is convicted of impaired driving causing bodily harm or impaired driving causing death, the court may impose, in addition to any other punishment, an order prohibiting the offender from operating a motor vehicle on any street, road, highway, or in any other public place, during a specified period of time.

If the offender is liable to imprisonment for life, the period of prohibition may be of any duration the court considers proper. If the offender is liable to imprisonment for more than five years but less than life, the order may cover any period not exceeding ten years, and in any other case, the period shall not exceed three years.

b. WHAT KIND OF EVIDENCE CAUSES POLICE TO STOP A VEHICLE?

Erratic driving is the most obvious reason why police are attracted to a suspected impaired driver. Driving behavior that attracts the police may include the following:

(a) Driving without headlights

(b) Weaving across lanes or over the centre line

(c) Hitting medians or abutments

(d) Any form of accident with a pedestrian or lamp post or building or other car

(e) Driving too slowly or too fast or speeding

(f) Going through red lights or stop signs

(g) Any kind of driving which may endanger pedestrians or other vehicles

(h) Any other form of erratic driving

An impaired driving case may begin with a report of erratic driving by a civilian to police. In many urban and rural areas of Canada, police frequently maintain a degree of surveillance on the parking lots and trunk roads near neighborhood pubs, hotel bars and beer parlors, nightclubs, legions, and so forth. In the past, this has proved a fruitful hunting ground for impaired driving suspects, particularly near the closing hours of such premises.

The routine check of vehicles in police roadblocks is another frequent source of suspects. This is becoming a particularly common practice in major Canadian cities during the Yule season and is probably a strong deterrent to impaired driving offences.

c. RIGHTS OF THE DRIVER WHO IS STOPPED AND QUESTIONED

Reference has been made to the legal requirements of a driver to carry and to produce to a police officer upon request the vehicle registration, insurance documents, and a driver's licence.

However, apart from identifying yourself, supplying these documents, and verifying your address, nothing else is required of you if you are the driver. There is no requirement that you give account of yourself, explain where you have been or whether you had anything to drink, or anything else. As in any other situation, the driver has the right to refuse to answer questions.

d. DO POLICE HAVE THE RIGHT TO SEARCH A SUSPECTED IMPAIRED DRIVER?

There are no "stop and frisk" laws in Canada such as would enable a police officer to do a routine pat down search of a driver of a motor vehicle who has been stopped for any suspected offence. The law permits the police officer to stop the vehicle and to establish the identification of the driver in the manner referred to above.

However, unless a charge is to be laid — it could be a traffic citation under provincial motor vehicle laws or a Criminal Code offence — the officer has no other powers. No driver is required to submit to a search of person unless he or she has been arrested.

Where police choose to arrest the driver for impaired driving, they have a right to search the driver as an incident to a lawful arrest. However, where there is merely a demand to accompany the officer to the station to give a breath sample, the courts have held that this is not necessarily an arrest. The mere fact that a demand has been made does not give police the right to search the suspect.

However, police also frequently arrest the accused for impaired driving, so that often there is both a demand to accompany for purposes of breathalyzer tests *and* an arrest.

Once an arrest for impaired driving is made, a police officer may wish to search the person to find alcohol, drugs, or weapons. Any drugs or other illegal items may be seized and charges laid.

e. SEARCH OF VEHICLE

There is nothing in the impaired driving laws that adds to the powers to search a motor vehicle. If the suspect consents to a search of the vehicle, police are entitled to pursue it. Otherwise, police are not entitled to search, and the owner is entitled to object to any attempt to search. A search could be carried out legally if an officer gives a legal reason, such as under provincial liquor laws (see chapter 16).

f. WHAT FACTORS MAY LEAD POLICE TO CHARGE A DRIVER?

Impaired driving cases are usually based on circumstantial evidence. There are several kinds of evidence that may lead police to be suspicious, or to lay a charge against a suspect. They include the following:

(a) Driving evidence
— reviewed above

(b) Physical observations
— alcohol on breath
— behavior showing faulty co-ordination (fumbling with wallet when trying to find driver's licence and other documents)

(c) Speech problems, such as slurring of words, repeating words, silly or nonsensical remarks made to the officer

(d) Bloodshot or watery eyes

(e) Poor balance, swaying when standing

(f) Staggering or leaning on the car or other objects for support

(g) Sloppy or disheveled appearance

(h) Belligerent attitude

(i) Any combination of the foregoing

g. PHYSICAL TESTS

There is no requirement by law to perform any physical tests when asked to do so by the police. The usual tests that are requested are the following:

(a) Standing with the head tilted back and eyes closed, arms out to the sides, and trying to touch the tip of the index finger to the nose

(b) Walking a straight line from heel to toe

(c) Picking up coins from the floor

(d) Standing on one leg and raising the other leg

h. STATEMENTS OF SUSPECTS

Any admission of drinking, or even a denial of drinking, may be evidence against the driver. In a court of law, a denial of drinking anything at all may be as problematic as an admission if there is clear evidence of an odor of liquor coming from the suspect's breath.

Drivers commonly claim they had only "two beer" or "a couple of drinks." Such statements are often detrimental to their case, especially on a .08 driving charge. The law in this area is frequently concerned with the scientific data relating to the rate at which alcohol is absorbed into the human body. In past cases where an accused has attempted to mislead a police officer by making a false statement in regard to the amount of alcohol consumed, it has rebounded on the accused and hurt the court case.

i. BREATHALYZER TESTS

Breathalyzer tests and the rights of a suspect who is requested to take such tests are discussed below. It is important to note that on a charge of impaired driving (as opposed to driving with more than .08 blood alcohol) the fact of refusing to take a breathalyzer test, if such refusal is without lawful excuse, can be used against the accused. The judge can draw an adverse inference from a refusal.

j. THE DEMAND FOR BREATHALYZER TESTS

A police officer can lawfully demand that a suspected impaired driver take a breathalyzer test if he or she believes on reasonable and probable grounds that the person is committing or has committed (within two hours) the offence of impaired driving or driving over .08.

The demand includes two things: first, to provide sufficient samples of breath to make the proper analysis and, second, to accompany the officer to a mobile breathalyzer unit or to the police station for that purpose.

All provinces also have a federal law permitting police to take a roadside screening test, known as an ALERT. For this test, police need establish only that they have a mere suspicion that you have alcohol in your body in order to demand breath samples. However, the ALERT test is not evidence against you on a later charge of driving with more than 80 milligrams of alcohol per 100 millilitres of blood, although a refusal to provide a sample for an ALERT test is an offence and just as severe as refusing to supply tests which could lead to a .08 charge.

k. BLOOD SAMPLES

By virtue of amendments to the Criminal Code, if a person is suspected of impaired driving or driving over .08, a police officer may in certain circumstances require that person to provide a blood sample. This provision is triggered where the police officer has reasonable and probable grounds to believe that by reason of any physical condition of the person, that person may be incapable of providing a sample of his breath or it would be impracticable to obtain a sample of his breath.

Only a qualified medical practitioner or a qualified technician under the direction of a qualified medical practitioner may take the samples, and that qualified person must accompany the police officer for the purpose of taking such samples. A sample may not be taken where to do so would endanger the life or health of the person. This section is resorted to where there has been a motor vehicle accident, and the accused person has been injured and is in the care of a physician at a hospital.

Samples may only be taken where a justice has issued a telewarrant or other warrant to a police officer authorizing a qualified medical practitioner or technician to take the samples of blood and a copy of the warrant must be served as soon as practicable on the person from whom the blood sample is taken. The information on oath required to obtain the warrant includes a statement setting out the offence alleged to have been committed and identifying the person from whom the blood sample is to be taken. Some courts have held the accused person is entitled to have an expert witness conduct his or her tests on the blood sample to determine whether that sample was properly taken and properly reflects the analysis that has been set out in the certificate.

l. RIGHT TO A LAWYER

You have the right to consult with a lawyer before taking breathalyzer tests which will lead potentially to a charge of over .08 driving. Many people are uncertain of their rights and validly desire information on whether police have the grounds to require them to take the test. They may have been arrested outside of their vehicle or in a situation where the vehicle was not road worthy or where they had no intention of driving or may have given care and control of the vehicle to some sober person at some earlier time.

Many situations could arise where a person justifiably wants legal advice before providing breath samples which might provide incriminating evidence. The accused has a constitutional right to retain and instruct counsel without delay. Police are under a duty to tell you of that right if you are arrested or detained. If you assert this right, police are under the legal obligation to give you a reasonable opportunity to consult with counsel.

This normally means giving you the opportunity to use a telephone and to consult counsel in private. Refusal to provide a telephone or privacy in the phone call with counsel may provide a reasonable excuse for refusing to take the breathalyzer tests.

The opportunity to consult counsel must be reasonable, which normally means that a telephone and a telephone book and a reasonable number of phone calls to reach a lawyer must be made available. Provided the right to counsel is being asserted in a legitimate and bona fide manner, the courts will tolerate no abridgement, restriction, refusal, or denial of the right.

However, a word of caution is needed here. An accused person who does not seriously pursue the right to counsel and who is obviously stalling the police or is acting as though everything is a big joke will not find much sympathy with the court if the police abridge the right to counsel. The right to consult a lawyer is a very cherished and important right in Canadian law and should be exercised in a serious manner.

Where police have demanded that you accompany them to provide breathalyzer tests, under Section 238 of the Criminal Code you have the right to consult a lawyer and to be advised of this right. Failure to advise you of this right or to permit reasonable opportunity to consult counsel will usually be a defence to a charge of refusing to provide breath samples. If breath samples are obtained by police as a result of violation of these constitutional rights, the court will usually reject the evidence of the breathalyzer results.

In some circumstances, it may be reasonable to contact a friend or family member and have that person contact a lawyer and have the lawyer phone you back at the police station. However, if you are not contacting the lawyer directly and you are employing one of these other methods to reach the lawyer, and it is reasonable in the circumstances, you should advise the police of what you are doing so that they do not think you are simply wasting time.

Be aware that the right to retain and instruct counsel without delay does not apply to police requests for breath samples for the ALERT test. The Supreme Court of Canada has held that while a person is detained when asked by police to provide such a sample, and the right to counsel arises at the moment of detention, that due to the practical considerations of operating the roadside screening devices, and the purpose for which the legislation exists, that the effective denial of the right to counsel in such circumstances is a justifiable limit of rights under Section 1 of the Charter.

It is important to realize that the ALERT test is really a pre-test. Even if a person failed it by blowing over .08, the evidence would not be proof on a .08 charge. The accused would still have the right to consult counsel after providing the ALERT sample, but before providing breathalyzer samples that could be used on a .08 driving charge.

Whenever you are asked to provide samples of breath under Section 238 of the Criminal Code which could be used to support a .08 driving charge, you would be wise to request the opportunity to consult a lawyer or to have some legal counsel.

16
THE LIQUOR LAWS

The manufacture, possession, purchase, sale, and consumption of alcohol in Canada is tightly controlled by interlocking federal and provincial laws. The manufacture and use of alcohol provides a substantial revenue source for each level of government.

Federal laws contained in the Excise Act and the Excise Tax Act set out licensing requirements for distillers and producers of alcoholic spirits or beer and for the payment of excise taxes on these items. The act creates extraordinary powers of search and seizure to ensure compliance with licensing requirements and payment of duties or tax.

Retail marketing, sale, and consumption of beer and spirit alcohol products, as well as the production and sale of domestic wine, is governed by provincial law under which there are also wide powers of search and seizure.

a. BEER AND WINE PRODUCED FOR PERSONAL USE

1. Beer and cider

There is an exemption from excise duties in the case of beer brewed by a person for his or her sole use or the use of family members living in the same residence, providing the beer is not sold to these people. However, the Excise Act requires that you give written notice to the nearest Revenue collector before beginning to brew. Any sale or other unauthorized dealing with beer is an offence under federal law and will be a separate offence under provincial law.

Provincial laws also permit the manufacture of beer and cider for personal consumption.

2. Wine

Provincial laws permit the manufacture of wine for personal use without compliance with the usual licensing requirements.

b. LIQUOR OFFENCES UNDER FEDERAL REVENUE LAWS

All manufacturing of spirit alcohol or beer (except for personal use, as above) is illegal unless done with a federal licence under the Excise Act.

It is an offence to possess any equipment, such as a still or any brewery apparatus except with proper compliance with the licensing requirements. Any such equipment and any unlawfully produced liquor can be seized by Revenue officers and forfeited to the Crown. A person carrying on business with unlicensed equipment may be charged.

Additionally, anyone who sells, offers to sell, purchases, or possesses any unlawfully manufactured or imported spirits, or spirits unlawfully moved, may be charged with an offence carrying a fine (between $100 and $200) or imprisonment for three to twelve months, or both. The spirits and any vehicle or vessel used to transport them may be seized and forfeited.

It is also an offence to brew for sale any beer or malt liquor or to possess any without a proper licence. This is also an offence carrying fines and possible jail terms.

c. SEARCH AND SEIZURE UNDER FEDERAL LIQUOR LAWS

Writs of assistance are no longer available to revenue collectors and officers under the Excise Act, having been found to be contrary to the right to be secure against unreasonable search or seizure under the Charter.

An ordinary search warrant must now be obtained from a justice of the peace. This procedure requires a revenue collector getting a sworn affidavit setting out "reasonable grounds" for the search. A search warrant can authorize a search of any specified house, building or place, with the search to be carried out between sunrise and sunset.

d. OFFENCES UNDER PROVINCIAL LIQUOR LAWS

The distribution and retail sale of liquor is governed by provincial laws. It is unlawful to possess, purchase, or sell liquor except in accordance with provincial licensing and retail requirements. These laws vary somewhat from province to province. The offences are summary and usually result in a fine for a first conviction. They include the following:

(a) Illegal sale of liquor or possession for the purpose of illegal sale ("bootlegging" is the common term)

(b) Purchasing liquor otherwise than through authorized retail channels

(c) Supplying liquor to a minor. Supplying liquor to a minor is a serious matter. The only time a minor can legally drink is when the liquor is supplied by a parent or guardian at home.

(d) Sale of liquor to a minor in a licensed premises or at a store (there is a defence where the vendor has requested identification and has carefully and prudently verified the authenticity of it)

(e) Being a minor in a liquor store, lounge, or pub, or a minor purchasing, possessing, or consuming liquor

(f) Consuming liquor or being drunk in a public place

e. SEARCH AND SEIZURE UNDER PROVINCIAL LIQUOR LAWS

Police acting under provincial liquor laws may search automobiles without a warrant. They need only a reasonable suspicion that the automobile contains illegal liquor or that liquor is kept in the automobile for an unlawful purpose.

In most provinces, they can also search a person's land, except for dwelling houses, without a warrant. These laws also permit them to search people found in a car, or on land, where liquor violations are suspected. However, it should be noted that some of the provincial legislation has been successfully challenged in the lower courts.

Under the liquor laws, police officers need a warrant to search a dwelling. To obtain the warrant they must have reasonable grounds for believing that a liquor violation is occurring in the dwelling, but they need not give reasons for their suspicion or belief. A warrant enables officers to enter any part of the building.

There are variations in the laws in various provinces. In Manitoba, for example, police searching a building or premises may require found-ins to give their names and addresses. In Ontario, police may search people in a place they have entered with a warrant. However, in British Columbia, you may not be searched until you have been arrested.

The rules for objecting to searches under provincial liquor laws are the same as for other searches. Police must state a reason for the search. You should demand to see the warrant. Check it to see that it specifies your house and yourself, and that it bears the proper dates. If it is accurate, let the police in. You may make notes of their activities, and you may refuse to answer questions until you talk to a lawyer.

17
SEARCH AND SEIZURE UNDER THE CUSTOMS LAWS: BORDER SEARCHES

Our country has strict rules governing the importation of goods from elsewhere. These rules are found in the Customs Act and are administered by Revenue Canada — Customs and Excise.

The primary object of customs laws is the protection of Canadian industry from international competitors. The practical effect of the duties imposed on most imported goods is that they ensure that the Canadian retailer and consumer will not benefit economically from purchasing products from a foreign source at a price less than that which they could be bought for in Canada.

An additional function of the customs laws is to prevent smuggling. Smuggling can be undertaken in an effort to circumvent the payment of customs duties on imported goods, or for the purpose of importing illegal goods, such as narcotics.

From a civil rights point of view, the key is that no one has a right to bring anything into Canada that has been obtained elsewhere without declaring it to a customs officer. In most cases, after payment of proper duties, the item will be admitted into the country.

Every permanent resident is entitled once in each calendar year to import $300 in goods from another country without payment of duties after a seven day absence.

Also, after any 48-hour absence from Canada, you are entitled to bring into the country duty free goods totalling $100 which can include 1.1 litres (40 oz.) of liquor or wine or 8.2 litres (288 oz.) of beer or ale, 200 cigarettes, 50 cigars, and .91 kilograms (2 lbs.) of tobacco.

a. ARRIVING AT THE CANADIAN BORDER

People arriving at the Canadian border, including both Canadians returning to Canada and visitors to this country, can expect to be stopped by immigration officers (dealt with in the next chapter) and customs officers.

People entering Canada must do so legally and can bring with them only what the law allows. Immigration officials are empowered to question arrivals as to their legal right to enter, that is, whether they are Canadian citizens, landed immigrants, holders of visitors' visas, or on a short holiday from the United States.

Immigration officials are also entitled to inspect passports or other identification documents to confirm the right to enter.

The Customs Act gives customs officers very wide powers to regulate importing and to investigate smuggling. Every person in charge of a vehicle or vessel arriving in Canada, or a person arriving on foot, must go to the nearest custom house to make a report in writing to the collector or proper officer at the custom house of all goods in his or her control or in the vehicle and any fittings, furnishings, or parts of the vehicle.

You are also required to answer questions regarding articles to be brought into the country. This process is referred to as making "due entry" of the articles as required by law.

Failure to do so is an offence and will lead to the forfeiture of the goods and the vehicle in which they have been imported. It can also subject the person responsible to fines and imprisonment.

b. SEARCH OF PERSON

Although there are wide powers to search vehicles and baggage, there is some restriction on the right of customs officers to search individuals. In order to make a person search the customs officer must have *reasonable cause* to suppose that the person to be searched has goods subject to entry at customs, or prohibited goods, secreted about his or her person.

A customs officer who has such reasonable cause is entitled to search anyone on board any vessel or boat or in any vehicle entering Canada by land or in-land navigation, or any person who has landed or come out of such vessel, boat or vehicle.

Note that the definition of vehicle under the Customs Act includes everything from chuckwagons to aircraft. With reasonable cause a customs officer can search anyone who has come into Canada from a foreign country in any manner whatsoever.

If you feel you are being harassed by a customs officer, you may require the officer to take you before a police magistrate or justice of the peace or before the collector or chief officer at the port or entry place. Any of the persons mentioned has power to evaluate the claim for reasonable cause for the search.

If the magistrate or other person does not agree that there is reasonable cause for the search, you may be discharged. If the customs officer's point of view is accepted, the magistrate can direct that you be searched. The act specifically provides that a person must be searched by a person of the same sex.

The act sets out extensive protection for customs officers who may be potentially sued for civil liability, and requires that any action must be commenced within three months of the cause of action arising.

c. **SEARCH OF BAGGAGE AND VEHICLE**

The act provides that customs officers may, upon information or upon reasonable grounds of suspicion, detain, open, and examine any package suspected to contain prohibited property or smuggled goods or goods involved in a violation of the act.

They are entitled to board and enter any vessel or vehicle, including aircraft of any description whatsoever and may stop and detain any vehicle whether arriving from places beyond or within the limits of Canada and may rummage and search all parts of it for goods.

If any goods are found in any vehicle or vessel, the customs officer may seize and secure the vessel, together with all its rigging and anything else attached to it, plus all the goods or things it is carrying.

It will be at once apparent that this is a very wide search power in that no search warrant is required and a search can be made on the basis of mere suspicion, although that suspicion is required to be based on reasonable grounds.

d. SEARCH OF A BUILDING OR WAREHOUSE

Customs officers are required to swear on oath before a justice of the peace that they have reasonable cause to suspect that goods liable to forfeiture are in any particular building, yard, or other place before they can make such search.

Having done this, they are entitled to enter any building, warehouse, or other place between sunrise and sunset. If the doors are fastened, they are required by the act to demand admission, including declaring the purpose for which they wish entry. If admission is not given, customs officers are entitled to enter forcibly.

Once entry is made, they are entitled to search the premises and seize all goods that they have reasonable grounds to believe are subject to forfeiture. If no justice of the peace resides in the place where the search is to be carried out, it can be carried out without the oath or the assistance of a justice of the peace.

e. WRITS OF ASSISTANCE

Writs of assistance similar to those formerly available to narcotics officers are no longer available to customs officers.

However, where it is not practicable to obtain a search warrant, customs officers are still entitled to enter at any time of day or night into any building or other place within their jurisdiction. They may search for and seize any goods that they have reasonable grounds to believe are liable to forfeiture under the act, and they are entitled to break open doors, chests, or packages, if necessary, to make their search.

f. ARREST WITHOUT A WARRANT

Customs officers are entitled to arrest without a warrant anyone found committing or suspected of having committed any indictable offence under the Customs Act or under the Criminal Code, whether or not the offence is in connection with customs matters.

g. SEIZURE AND FORFEITURE OF GOODS

There is a general power of seizure and forfeiture of any goods that are illegally imported into Canada and every person involved in such unlawful importation incurs a penalty equal to the value of the goods.

In addition to these penalties, there may also be charges of summary or indictable offences under the Customs Act, depending on whether the value of the goods is under or over $1 000. In both cases, the offences are punishable by minimum fines or imprisonment or both.

h. SEIZURE AND FORFEITURE OF VEHICLE

Any vessels or vehicles and all things attached to them are liable to seizure and forfeiture under the act if they have been used in the importation, shipping, landing, or transportation of any goods liable to forfeiture.

Everyone who has assisted in the removal of the goods is liable to forfeit a sum of money equal to the value of the goods and also liable to criminal prosecution by summary or indictable offence, depending on the value of the goods.

There is a right to appeal to the deputy minister responsible for Revenue Canada concerning seizure and forfeiture of a vehicle or goods. The deputy minister may decide to release the item on terms (such as payment of penalty) or may refer the matter to a court. If you, as owner or claimant, are not satisfied with the deputy minister's decision, you have the right to notify him or her within 30 days that the decision will not be accepted and the deputy minister may then refer the matter to the court.

Any person whose vehicle or goods has been seized as forfeited under the act or anyone who claims an interest in the vehicle or goods may apply within 60 days after the seizure by notice in writing to a judge for an order declaring his or her interest. Either the Crown or the claimant may appeal the decision of the court to the court of appeal.

i. AIRPORT SEARCHES

Security requirements at airports regularly involve the x-ray of luggage and hand baggage for weapons. The purposes of these searches are to find contraband that may be smuggled, such as drugs or weapons, to prevent hijackings, and so on. In most cases, the searches are perfunctory perusals of luggage and handbags.

There are stop and frisk searches of passengers on the basis of the merest suspicion that some metal item that could be a gun is being carried. More comprehensive searches, such as strip searches, rectal, or vaginal examinations are not permitted. This kind of search could only be justified if done by police officers in circumstances where it was probable that a crime was being committed.

It is likely that the American rule would be followed so that there would have to be some "plain suggestion" of criminal activity, for example, a search for narcotics where a person appears to be high on drugs and has a record for narcotics use. A less thorough search of luggage, clothing, packages, or vehicles has in most instances to date been found lawful in our courts. However, there have been circumstances where the courts have held that the lack of reasonable and probable grounds to conduct the search means that even minimal intrusion is unconstitutional.

In general, the whole area of airport searches is an unclear area of law, and there is no legal authority as to the allowable extent of these routine searches. It is fairly certain that judges would require reasonable grounds for any more detailed sort of search of passengers.

18
IMMIGRATION LAWS: TOURISTS AND VISITORS

Canada's borders are generally open to tourists and visitors. However, immigration officers have wide discretionary powers and, despite the general permission for tourists and visitors to enter, many are held up or turned away.

In general, a visitor to Canada is not required to apply for a visa before appearing at a port of entry on Canada's borders. No one is required to obtain a visa in advance if their intention is only to be in transit through Canada for not more than four days. In addition, all permanent residents of the United States are allowed to arrive at a border point to request visitor rights without obtaining a visa.

Citizens of many other countries in South America, Africa, Europe, and Asia are also permitted to apply for a visa at a port of entry. This right is accorded to all citizens of the United Kingdom and British subjects. It is also available to members of a crew seeking shore leave or some other legitimate and temporary purpose, members of armed forces of members of the North Atlantic Treaty Organization (NATO) with identification documents and with Canadian consent relevant to movement of personnel between member states.

People ordinarily resident in the Soviet Union and other Euro-communist countries, China, Egypt, Saudi Arabia, Morocco, Lebanon, Syria, Iran, Iraq, and Zimbabwe are not permitted under Canadian immigration law to apply for entry at a port of entry. They must make application for a visa in the country of origin or at a Canadian embassy or consulate in another country.

a. WHO MAY NOT VISIT?

People who are not entitled to visit Canada include the following:

(a) People under health disability

(b) People unable or unwilling to support themselves

(c) People convicted of an indictable offence

(d) People convicted of two or more summary offences arising from separate incidents

(e) People engaging in espionage or subversion against democratic government as understood in Canada

(f) People who it is believed will engage in or instigate subversion by force of any government while in Canada

(g) People who there are reasonable grounds to believe will engage in acts of violence that might endanger the lives or safety of people in Canada

(h) People who it is believed will commit an indictable offence or engage in organized crime

(i) People who are not genuine visitors

A senior immigration officer may grant visitor rights for up to 30 days to people who have committed an indictable offence or the equivalent of an indictable offence for which the maximum penalty would have been less than 10 years, and to people who have committed two or more summary offences or offences that would be the equivalent of summary offences if committed in Canada.

In addition, people who would be inadmissible as a result of a criminal record may demonstrate that they have rehabilitated themselves and, in the case of an offence for which a term of imprisonment of ten years or more could have been imposed in Canada, at least five years have elapsed since the termination of the sentence that was imposed.

For lesser criminal offences, the proposed visitor may satisfy the Canadian government that he or she has been rehabilitated and that a period of five years has elapsed since the termination of the sentence, or, in the case of a person under twenty-one years of age, two years have elapsed since the termination of the sentence.

A person planning a visit to Canada who is uncertain about being admissible would be wise to make prior contact with a Canadian embassy or consulate to get advice and take steps to ease the entry once arriving at the border. Sometimes visits to Canada for a special meeting or other purpose can be frustrated by delays in crossing the border.

b. VISIT BY MINISTERIAL PERMIT

A ministerial permit may be issued in special cases authorizing a person who is a member of an inadmissible class to visit Canada. Such permit cannot be in force for longer than 12 months and can be cancelled at any time. The minister in charge of the Immigration Act may extend the permit.

No ministerial permit can be issued to a person against whom a removal order or departure notice has been issued and is outstanding.

c. WHAT MAY IMMIGRATION OFFICERS DEMAND?

Immigration officers at the border points will question visitors on their country of origin and citizenship. The officers can demand proof of identification and financial capability for the duration of the Canadian visit.

People who are not American citizens will be required to produce travel documents, including a passport. If you cannot show financial responsibility, you can be refused entry on the basis that you might become a charge on the state.

In addition, as was explained in the previous chapter, customs officers at the borders of Canada have wide powers to search automobiles and people for contraband goods at the border. If you are in possession of anything illegal, you may be refused entry or arrested, charged, and later deported. Obviously, if you want to come into Canada, you should comply with certain fundamentals:

(a) Carry identification documents (including a passport)
(b) Have a definite travel plan
(c) Have financial capability
(d) Dress appropriately
(e) Do not carry contraband

d. STUDENT AND WORK VISAS

Non-immigrants are sometimes allowed into Canada to study or work. To enter Canada for a specific length of time to work or study, you must produce documentation in the form of student or work visas or authorizations.

If you hope to work or study in Canada, you should know that you must make application for an authorization to study or work to a visa officer outside of Canada. These authorizations are not granted at a port of entry on Canada's borders.

This rule holds for anyone who intends to apply to immigrate to Canada as a permanent resident. There is an exception in the case of people who are the spouse or unmarried son or daughter of a diplomat or other representative of another country, a member of a military force coming to Canada for a purpose in connection with defence or security interests of Canada, a member of the clergy coming to carry out religious duties, an employee of a foreign news reporting company coming to report on Canadian events, or a person coming to engage in an athletic activity.

e. MEDICAL EXAMINATIONS

Any visitor who seeks to be employed in Canada for a period of longer than 90 days must undergo a required medical examination. This can include a mental examination, a physical examination, and an assessment of medical records.

Such people must possess a valid certificate of medical assessment certifying that they are not persons who suffer from a disease, disability, or disorder such that they may be a danger to the public health or safety or make excessive demands on health or social services.

f. GROUPS OF PERFORMERS AND ATHLETES

Large groups of performers and the entourages of performers (parties of 20 people or more) are exempt from the requirement to have an employment authorization. This exemption also applies to a foreign news reporter covering Canadian events and to members of athletic teams entering to engage in sports activities.

However, groups of performers and other persons who may enter without employment authorization must not engage in any secondary employment unless they obtain an employment authorization.

g. TEMPORARY VISITS OF BUSINESS REPRESENTATIVES

A representative of a foreign business or government coming to Canada for the purpose of purchasing goods or services is permitted to enter without employment authorization.

Similarly, representatives of a foreign business or a foreign government coming to Canada for less than 90 days for the purpose of selling goods are permitted to enter without an employment authorization, provided that that representative is not engaged in selling to the general public or to people who operate retail outlets.

An employee of a corporation, union, or other organization operating outside of Canada coming into Canada for less than 90 days to consult with other employees or members, or to inspect a Canadian parent or subsidiary corporation or branch office of the union, is permitted to enter without an employment authorization.

h. EMPLOYMENT AUTHORIZATIONS

Employment authorizations may be denied on the basis that employment of the visitor will adversely affect the employment opportunities for Canadians or Canadian permanent residents.

The immigration officer will consider whether a prospective employer has made reasonable efforts to hire or train

Canadians for the employment, the qualifications of the applicant, and whether the wages or working conditions offered are sufficient to attract and retain Canadian citizens or residents.

An employment authorization can be issued to a person coming into Canada under a contract to fulfil a single or continuous guest entertainment in the performing arts except where the engagement is merely incidental to commercial activity that does not limit itself to artistic presentation, or it constitutes employment in a permanent position in a Canadian organization.

The requirement of looking for a Canadian to fill the job can be dispensed with if the employment of the alien person will create or maintain significant employment opportunities for Canadians, or the person is to be employed by a religious or charitable organization, or the employment would result in reciprocal employment of Canadians abroad.

It is illegal for anyone who is not a Canadian citizen, a landed immigrant to Canada, or anyone who does not have a ministerial permit or a valid employment visa, to work in Canada. If you work illegally in Canada, you will be deported. To enter Canada for employment, you must produce documentation to Canadian immigration authorities.

Students need documentation proving acceptance into a course of studies from a Canadian university or other program. A student or work visa is only valid for the period of study or work specified. Unless the stay is extended by ministerial permit, the person must leave after the course of study is finished.

i. WHO MAY BE DEPORTED?

A visitor or tourist who commits a crime in Canada and is taken to a Canadian prison will automatically be detained under an "immigration hold."

This means that even if the person is acquitted of the criminal charge, Canadian immigration authorities will nevertheless hold an inquiry to determine if the person is legally in Canada, and whether a removal order or departure notice (allowing voluntary departure) should be issued.

At this stage, the immigration authorities are entitled to look at any criminal record the person had before arriving in Canada. If the person was granted landing subject to terms and conditions and has violated those, is engaged in or instigating subversion by force of the Canadian government or any government, has been convicted of any offence in Canada for which a period of imprisonment of more than six months has been imposed or for which five years or more could have been imposed, he or she may be deported.

Similarly, if you are granted landing by reason of false passport or visa documents or documents obtained by misrepresentation of material facts, or have wilfully failed to support yourself or your family, you can be arrested. An inquiry can be held and a removal order made.

A visitor who has engaged in employment unlawfully, engaged in subversion by force of any government, been convicted of any offence under the Criminal Code, remained after the visitor visa expired, failed to report at a port of entry upon arrival at the Canadian border, or used false documents, is also subject to arrest, inquiry, and removal order if an adjudicator finds the allegations made out.

j. RIGHT OF DETAINED PERSON TO HAVE LEGAL COUNSEL AND INTERPRETER

Any person who is detained or who is otherwise the subject of an immigration inquiry has the right to legal counsel and the right to an interpreter if he or she does not have a sufficient grasp of the language.

These rights are fundamental and guaranteed in the statute and in the Constitution. In addition, there is a right of appeal from an inquiry by an adjudicator to the federal court of appeal. The act provides for an application for bail or release pending the hearing of the appeal.

19
IMMIGRATION, POLITICAL ASYLUM, AND EXTRADITION

a. IMMIGRATING TO CANADA

You cannot immigrate from within Canada. It is not possible to apply for a visa from within Canada, nor is it possible to apply for landed status from within Canada. These applications must be made outside of Canada. They can be made to immigration authorities at Canadian consulates or diplomatic embassies. An exception arises in the case of a person married to a Canadian citizen, who may be sponsored as an immigrant by that spouse and may then apply from within Canada.

b. WHO MAY NOT IMMIGRATE?

People in certain "inadmissible classes" are forbidden from immigrating to Canada. These include the following:

(a) People suffering from certain infectious or contagious diseases, mental or physical disability, or other health impairment

(b) People who are unable or unwilling to support themselves and those dependent on them, unless they have satisfied an immigration officer that adequate arrangements have been made for their care and support

(c) People convicted of an offence that would be equivalent in Canada to an indictable offence carrying a maximum term of ten years' imprisonment or more, unless they have rehabilitated themselves to the satisfaction of the federal cabinet and at least five years have expired since the end of the sentence

(d) People who there are reasonable grounds to believe will commit indictable offences or engage in organized crime

(e) People who have engaged in or who there are reasonable grounds to believe will engage in acts of espionage or subversion against democratic government as understood in Canada, unless they can satisfy the Minister of Employment and Immigration that their admission would not be detrimental to the national interest even though they engaged in such acts in the past

(f) People who there are reasonable grounds to believe will engage in or instigate the subversion by force of any government

(g) People who there are reasonable grounds to believe will engage in acts of violence that might endanger the lives or safety of people in Canada or are likely to participate in unlawful activities of an organization likely to engage in acts of violence

(h) People who are not genuine immigrants or visitors

A person who is a member of an inadmissible class may be permitted to enter or remain in Canada on a ministerial permit. However, as mentioned in reference to visitors and tourists, a ministerial permit is an exceptional procedure and it is not available to a person against whom there is an existing removal order or departure notice.

c. ARREST AND BAIL

A person arrested by immigration authorities and held for an inquiry may be permitted to have bail. There is a right to be represented by a lawyer at the inquiry. Where a removal order is made, there may be a right to appeal to the Immigration Appeal Board or to the federal court of appeal.

Visitors and tourists against whom a removal order is made (that is, any person who has no special status, permit, or visa) have no right of appeal.

However, you may have a right to appeal to the Immigration Appeal Board if you are —

(a) A permanent resident

(b) A person seeking admission as an immigrant

(c) A non-immigrant who possesses a valid immigration visa or non-immigrant visa issued outside Canada by an immigration officer

(d) A political refugee seeking asylum

(e) A person who claims to be a Canadian citizen

While your appeal is pending, the board may grant you bail with terms or conditions.

d. POLITICAL ASYLUM AND EXTRADITION

1. Asylum

The Minister of Employment and Immigration can grant political asylum to refugees from foreign countries. A person seeking refugee status in Canada who is denied political asylum has a right to appeal to the Immigration Appeal Board. This board has the power to grant entrance or landing as well as to stay or quash an order of deportation if there are grounds for believing that deportation will result in punishment for political activities or other unusual hardship.

2. Wanted criminals

People wanted for crimes committed in other countries may be returned to those countries by Canada under the Fugitive Offenders Act (which applies to Commonwealth countries) or the Extradition Act (which applies to non-Commonwealth countries, including the United States).

These acts provide for the arrest of "wanted persons" in Canada and a hearing to determine if there is sufficient evidence against them. If there is sufficient evidence, they are held in custody pending surrender to the foreign country.

3. The extradition hearing

At an extradition hearing the judge must receive evidence tending to prove that the "wanted person" is not being extradited for political offences or that the foreign country has taken the proceedings in order to punish the person for political offences.

If there is sufficient evidence to justify a trial in Canada, or that would justify conviction in Canada (if the person is being sought for a sentence), the judge will issue a warrant of committal to hold the person in custody for surrender to the foreign country.

There is a right of appeal that must be taken within 15 days following committal for surrender. If there is insufficient evidence for committal, the judge will discharge the accused.

The Minister of Justice has power to refuse to surrender a fugitive if it appears that the offence is political or that the proceedings are for the purpose of prosecuting or punishing the person for political offences. No person can be legally extradited for political offences.

Canada may also demand extradition of persons back to Canada when they have committed a crime in Canada and fled.

e. CANADIANS TRAVELLING TO FOREIGN COUNTRIES

It is impossible to outline all the relevant rules and regulations that Canadians travelling to foreign countries will want to know.

In the case of the United States (and many other foreign countries), the border regulations are very similar to the regulations at the Canadian border. Visitors and tourists are allowed in. It is helpful if your apparel and manner are appropriate, your stated purpose is an acceptable one (a travel itinerary is desirable), you have necessary identification documents, and you can show financial capability for the duration of your intended visit.

If you have refugee status in Canada, but do not have a Canadian passport, and want to travel to the United States and other foreign countries, you must obtain refugee travel documents. In particular, this includes a certificate of identity from the Department of External Affairs. In addition, you will generally need a visa from authorities in the country you plan to visit.

Note: For detailed, step-by-step information about how to immigrate to Canada, see *Immigrating to Canada*, another title in the Self-Counsel Legal Series.

20
THE WEAPONS LAWS

A high degree of regulation and control characterizes Canada's laws on the possession and use of firearms and other weapons. The Canadian government takes a dim view of an individual being armed except for the purpose of hunting game. There is no basic right to keep a weapon even for the purpose of self-defence.

Our neighbors in the United States have adopted a somewhat different theory. In fact, the American Bill of Rights guarantees the right of the people to keep and bear arms.

a. IS THERE A RIGHT TO POSSESS FIREARMS?

There is no absolute right to possess firearms under the Criminal Code. Anyone who wishes legally to acquire a firearm must be the holder of a "firearms acquisition certificate." This will be issued by a firearms officer under the Criminal Code, or it may be a hunting licence or certificate or permit issued by a province where the same conditions have been complied with.

The term firearm in the Criminal Code is defined as any barrelled weapon from which any shot, bullet, or other missile can be discharged and that is capable of causing serious bodily injury or death to a person, and includes any frame or receiver of such a barrelled weapon and anything that can be adapted for use as a firearm. It is clear then that this definition includes any form of revolver or handgun, and any shotgun or rifle.

In provinces where the usual hunting permit does not qualify as the firearms acquisition certificate, an application must be made to a firearms officer. The officer will grant the right to acquire and possess a firearm provided there is nothing that raises a concern for the public or the applicant. In addition, no firearms acquisition certificate can be issued to a person under 16 years of age.

If you are refused a certificate, you may appeal to a magistrate, who may confirm or vary the decision of the firearms officer.

Most people will have no difficulty obtaining a certificate unless they have been convicted of an offence involving violence against another person or a weapons offence, or have had treatment for a mental disorder or have a history of violent behavior. In each of these cases, where the incident occurred within five years preceding the application, there will be a presumption that it is not in the interests of the applicant or other persons that he or she possess a firearm.

b. REVOLVERS (RESTRICTED WEAPONS)

Any firearm (except one that is a prohibited weapon, dealt with below) which is designed, altered, or intended to be aimed and fired by the action of one hand, such as revolvers, and any firearm that has a barrel of less than 46 centimetres in length and is capable of discharging centre-fire ammunition in a semi-automatic manner, or that folds or telescopes to a length of less than 65 centimetres and is adapted to be fired at that length, is a *restricted weapon*. This means that is unlawful to be in possession of such weapon except with a registration certificate for the weapon.

A restricted weapon registration certificate is also required for the following weapons: semi-automatic carbines known as commando mark 3; auto-loading 12 gauge shotgun, high standard model 10 series A or high standard model 10 series B; semi-automatic action rifle known as commando mark V; semi-automatic action rifle known as Thompson model 27A-1; and semi-automatic action rifle known as Colt model AR-15.

In the case of all these restricted weapons, a person found in possession of one must be able to produce then and there a registration certificate.

Possession of a restricted weapon without a registration certificate may be an indictable offence carrying imprisonment of up to five years or a summary conviction offence. In addition, where a police officer finds a person in possession of a restricted weapon and that person cannot produce a registration certificate, the officer is entitled to seize the weapon. If this occurs, the owner of the weapon may claim it within 14 days by producing the proper registration certificate. A registration certificate requires you to keep the weapon at your dwelling or place of business, as the case may be.

Requirements for a registration certificate for a restricted weapon are that you are the holder of a firearms acquisition certificate and are 18 or more years of age, that the weapon has distinct serial numbers, that it is required by you to protect life or for use in connection with your lawful profession or occupation, or for use in target practice through a shooting club or in accordance with conditions attached to a permit.

Gun collectors are entitled to possess restricted weapons if they can prove they are bona fide gun collectors. Certain antique guns classed as relics can also be possessed.

c. PERMIT TO MOVE A RESTRICTED WEAPON

A permit is required in order to move a restricted gun from one location to another, and to possess it anywhere other than at the place specified in the certificate.

A permit to move the gun or possess it elsewhere will be granted if you can show that it is necessary to protect life, or that you want it for use in connection with your profession or occupation, for target practice, to carry it to the local registrar of firearms, or to carry on a business (when in the business of importing and selling guns or a pawn shop business and so forth).

In addition, a permit may be granted to a person under the age of 16 who hunts or traps as a way of life, or a youth between 12 and 16 for the purpose of target practice, game hunting, or instruction in the use of firearms. In the latter case, consent of a parent or guardian is required.

d. REFUSAL OR REVOCATION OF PERMIT OR CERTIFICATE

The RCMP commissioner who has responsibility for registration certificates and permits may revoke or refuse permits where he or she knows of evidence that may make it unsafe for the applicant to have a weapon. In such case, the person will be given a reasonable period of time to surrender the weapons, unless an appeal has been taken against the commissioner's ruling.

An appeal is to a magistrate within 30 days after the commissioner's decision. In these cases the person who appeals is a competent and compellable witness and can be cross-examined on the matters that concern the commissioner. There is a further appeal to the county or district court against the decision of the magistrate.

e. PROHIBITED WEAPONS

Certain firearms and other weapons are absolutely prohibited by law in Canada. There is no certificate or permit permitting temporary or conditional possession or use of these weapons. They are illegal to possess or use under any circumstances. Prohibited weapons include the following:

(a) Machine-guns or other weapons capable of firing bullets in rapid succession during one pressure of the trigger

(b) Sawed-off rifles and shotguns where the barrel is less than 46 centimetres in length or the overall length is less than 65 centimetres

(c) Silencers, or any device intended to muffle or stop the sound or report of a firearm

(d) Switchblade knives, including any knife that has a blade that opens automatically by gravity or centrifugal force or by hand pressure applied to a button or spring or other device on the handle of the knife (in this regard, many ordinary so-called "jack-knives" or "buckknives" can be flicked open by hand by some police weapons experts, particularly if the knife has seen lots of use. A buckknife that works in this manner may be illegal, although it was not purchased as a knife that flicks open).

(e) The "SSS-1 Stinger" and similar devices consisting of single shot 22 calibre weapons designed to fit in the palm of the hand or in a cigarette package and many other similar items.

f. POSSESSION OF A WEAPON FOR A DANGEROUS PURPOSE

There is some confusion about what qualifies as a weapon. The Criminal Code defines a weapon as anything that is designed to be used as a weapon, or anything that a person uses or intends to use as a weapon.

A butcher knife is an implement for cutting meat or bread until the person possessing it uses it for a weapon. If you threaten someone with a butcher knife it becomes a weapon. If you carry a butcher knife to the scene of a riot and there is no food to cut, the court might find that the circumstances are sufficient to permit an inference that you intended to use it as a weapon.

g. THE RIGHT TO SELF-DEFENCE

People who are unlawfully assaulted have a right to defend themselves by using force if they do not intend to cause death or bodily harm that is grievous. You must use no more force than is necessary to enable you to defend yourself.

It is justifiable to use force to defend yourself or anyone under your protection from assault provided no more force than is necessary to prevent the assault or a repetition of it is used.

You are entitled to defend your possession of a dwelling house by using as much force as is necessary to prevent anyone from forcibly breaking in or entering the dwelling house without lawful authority. The use of force is justified to prevent a trespass on the dwelling house or the real property, or to remove a trespasser, provided no more force than is necessary is used.

Similarly, if you are in possession of chattels or movable property of any kind, you are justified in preventing a trespasser from taking it or in getting it back from a trespasser who has taken it provided you do not strike or cause bodily harm to the trespasser. However, where a trespasser persists in committing the theft, he or she is deemed to commit an assault and the person who is in peaceful possession of the movable property is entitled to defend that possession provided no more force than is necessary is used.

However, there is not necessarily a right to arm yourself for the purpose of self-defence. In fact, the general view in Canadian law is that possession of a weapon for a purpose of self-defence may amount to the offence of possession of a weapon for a purpose dangerous to the public peace. This is an indictable offence carrying a maximum penalty of imprisonment for 10 years.

In cases where a person took possession of a weapon (or imitation of a weapon) for the purpose of self-defence when about to go into a situation where there would be a probable confrontation with some enemy, it has been held that it was possession of a weapon for a purpose dangerous to the public peace.

The law is aimed at preventing situations where one person may provoke a violent confrontation with another while claiming to be armed only in self-defence. The law imposes a certain duty on the citizen to take steps to avoid a violent confrontation, not merely to take up arms in case such confrontation might occur and then possibly invite a situation where a confrontation will occur. The better course under Canadian law is to notify the police.

21
LAW OF PUBLIC MEETINGS

a. FREEDOM OF ASSOCIATION AND PEACEFUL ASSEMBLY

The Charter of Rights and Freedoms guarantees the right of all Canadians to freedom of peaceful assembly and freedom of association. These rights are obviously interwoven with freedom of conscience and freedom of thought, belief, opinion and expression, including freedom of the press. They are the fundamental political civil liberties of a democratic society.

The right to associate and peacefully assemble includes the right to meet, to demonstrate, to protest, to educate other members of the public, and so on. All these processes are embodied in the right to associate and assemble freely. The right to dissent in a democratic society is dependent on the maintenance of these constitutional freedoms.

The exercise of these rights is governed by certain federal laws, the Criminal Code, and provincial and municipal laws (e.g., noise by-laws, parade permit laws, and so on). The courts are concerned with balancing the right to assemble and express views with the interest of the community in law and order.

Police maintain a close watch on any public assembly on the basis that the right to demonstrate or protest carries with it the responsibility of maintaining the public peace and not interfering with other people's property or rights.

b. CONSTITUTIONAL LIMITS ON FUNDAMENTAL FREEDOMS

A potential limitation on constitutional rights to peacefully assemble and to associate is in Section 1 of the Charter. It provides that the rights and freedoms guaranteed in the Charter are subject to "such reasonable limits prescribed by law as can be demonstrably justified in a free and democratic society." It is difficult to know exactly what is meant by these words, and it will take a few court decisions to provide some guidance on this. For example, would proclamation of the War Measures Act provide a "reasonable limit" which is prescribed by law and is "demonstrably justified" in a free and democratic society?

c. A FURTHER CONSTITUTIONAL LIMIT: THE OPTING OUT CLAUSE

As mentioned in chapter 1, Section 33 of the Charter of Rights and Freedoms allows Parliament or a provincial legislature to enact laws that will operate "notwithstanding a provision included in Section 2 or Sections 7 to 15 of the Charter." (See Appendix for full text of Charter.)

In effect, this means that a province can opt out of the fundamental freedoms and legal rights provisions of the Charter by simply making a declaration that a statute will operate regardless of any conflict with those freedoms and rights. The only restriction on the use of Section 33 to opt out of freedoms and rights is that it can only be done for five years and then must be renewed. It can only be renewed for a further period of five years. There is a degree of concern among civil libertarians that the existence of Section 33 could undermine the effectiveness of the Constitution and the Charter.

d. DEFINITION OF UNLAWFUL ASSEMBLY

An unlawful assembly is defined in law as a group of three or more persons who, intending to carry out a common purpose, have assembled in such manner or are conducting themselves so as to cause fear among the neighborhood that they will disturb the peace tumultuously or needlessly and without reasonable cause provoke other people to disturb the peace tumultuously.

An assembly that starts off as a lawful assembly may become an unlawful assembly if it begins to do any of the things mentioned above. Unlawful assembly is a summary offence carrying a maximum penalty of six months in jail or a $2 000 fine or both.

e. RIOTS

A riot is an unlawful assembly that has begun to disturb the peace tumultuously. Participating in a riot is an indictable offence and carries a maximum penalty of two years in jail.

A justice, mayor, sheriff, or a deputy of one of those who receives notice that 12 or more persons have unlawfully and riotously assembled together is required to go to that place, approach as near as safely possible and, if satisfied that a riot is in progress, command silence and state in a loud voice the following words, which are from the Riot Act:

> Her Majesty the Queen charges and commands all persons being assembled immediately to disperse and peaceably to depart to their habitations or to their lawful business upon the pain of being guilty of an offence for which, upon conviction, they may be sentenced to imprisonment for life. God Save the Queen.

Indeed, any act opposing, hindering or assaulting wilfully and with force a person who is reading the Riot Act is an indictable offence and, upon conviction, renders an individual liable to imprisonment for life. Failure to peaceably disperse and depart from the place where the proclamation is made within 30 minutes after it is made is also an indictable offence and upon conviction carries an maximum penalty of life imprisonment. Even if you have not heard the proclamation, but have reasonable ground to believe that it would have been made if some person had not hindered the person who was making it, you still must depart within 30 minutes or be liable to a similar offence.

Police officers have wide powers in riot situations. Every police officer is justified in using as much force as is believed in good faith and on reasonable and probable grounds necessary to suppress a riot, although the force must not be excessive compared with the danger of allowing the riot to continue.

Anyone is justified in obeying the order of a police officer to use force to suppress a riot if he or she acts in good faith and if the order is not manifestly unlawful. If police are not there, any person who in good faith and on reasonable and probable grounds believes that serious mischief will result from a riot before police attend is justified in using as much force as he or she believes is necessary, provided the force does not exceed the danger of the riot continuing.

Once the Riot Act has been read, police are under a duty to disperse or arrest people who do not comply with the proclamation.

f. DISTURBANCES

By far a more common charge than unlawful assembly or participating in a riot is that of causing a disturbance. It is a less complicated charge for police to prove because under the Criminal Code a police officer can testify that "unknown persons," not necessarily witnesses at the trial, appeared to be disturbed. This evidence can afford the basis for Crown proof that there was, in fact, a disturbance.

A disturbance can be caused by fighting, screaming, shouting, swearing, singing, using insulting or obscene language, being drunk, impeding or molesting other persons, exposing or exhibiting an indecent exhibition in a public place, loitering in a public place and obstructing persons who are there, disturbing the peace and quiet of the occupants of a dwelling house by discharging firearms, or acting disorderly in a public place.

The offence is committed only by a person who is not in a dwelling house and who causes the disturbance in or near a public place.

Like the charge of unlawful assembly, the charge of causing a disturbance is a summary offence. This means you can be arrested for the offence only if you are found committing it.

There is no right to a preliminary hearing, and the trial proceeds before a magistrate or provincial court judge. The maximum penalties are a $2 000 fine or six months in jail or both.

g. PICKETING

The right of trade unionists and others to form picket lines for the purpose of communicating information is part of the right of freedom of peaceful assembly and association. This right is guaranteed by Section 2 of the Charter of Rights and Freedoms.

The Criminal Code specifically provides that it is not an offence for a person to be at or near a place for the purpose only of obtaining or communicating information. Such acts do not constitute watching and "besetting" within the meaning of the Criminal Code. The Code provisions of watching and besetting are directed at intimidation tactics, such as using violence or threats of violence to compel a person to do something, or persistently following a person from place to place in a disorderly manner on a highway, or blocking or obstructing a highway. These are all summary conviction offences.

Where a lawful strike is in progress, trade unionists have a legal right to be at the premises of the employer to picket and to inform the public. This right is subject only to compliance with the Criminal Code provisions on unlawful disturbances and assemblies, and watching and besetting provisions.

Where an unlawful strike is in progress and picketing continues despite an injunction, there may be civil or criminal contempt proceedings initiated against picketers.

h. ARREST AT AN UNLAWFUL DISTURBANCE OR ASSEMBLY

On the occasions where a person is arrested in the course of a large disturbance or unlawful assembly or riot, some legal first aid would be very helpful. In the first place, it is obviously foolish to take any drugs, weapons, or alcohol to the scene of a large public meeting which may become unruly. If you are arrested for a charge of causing a disturbance, you could also be charged for any drugs or weapons you might have in your possession.

Under Canadian weapons laws, even a hunting knife may subject you to a charge of possession of a weapon for a purpose dangerous to the public peace. Possession of alcohol in public streets could bring charges under provincial liquor laws.

It is a criminal offence for any person without lawful excuse to have a weapon in his or her possession while attending or en route to attend a public meeting. This is a summary offence carrying a maximum penalty of six months in jail or a $2 000 fine or both. The Criminal Code defines a weapon as anything designed to be used as a weapon or anything that a person uses or intends to use as a weapon, which obviously can include anything that might be used as a club.

Occasionally, police will break up an unruly demonstration by making a large number of arrests. This may result in an innocent bystander being arrested. If this happens, depending on the circumstances, there may be no point in trying to explain your innocence to the arresting constable. He or she will be busy with the task of getting you into a police vehicle to be taken to the stationhouse.

Anyone who is emotionally involved in a demonstration and its objectives may be tempted to make rash statements in the heat of the moment. This is a temptation to be resisted at all costs. Talk to a lawyer first because police will record any statements they can recall, in the words in which they recall them, as soon as they can. Any such statements will be used against you in court.

Sometimes a youth might be arrested and taken to the adult holding prison. It is important to inform the police at the earliest possible opportunity that you are a youth.

If you resist arrest, you may possibly be charged with a more serious offence such as assaulting or obstructing a police officer.

If you believe police officers have acted without justification or have assaulted or wrongfully arrested you or another person, it is important to gather evidence. As soon as possible, obtain the identities (names and badge numbers) of the police officers involved and the names of any independent witnesses who will be important when you are either defending criminal charges or bringing civil suits for damages against the police.

i. POST-ARREST PROCEDURES

Another difficulty with mass arrests is that it may be difficult to get telephone time after being taken to the police station. Friends who know you have been arrested can assist by asking a lawyer to come to the police station to arrange bail or release. Otherwise, you will probably have to await your time on the telephone.

On charges of causing a disturbance or unlawful assembly, both of which are summary offences, there is no right to take fingerprints and photographs of the arrested persons.

However, on any charge relating to the Riot Act, police are entitled to take fingerprints and photographs, as this is indictable.

22
SEX AND THE LAW

a. STATUTORY RAPE

Statutory rape is committed when a male has intercourse with a female under the age of 16. The male may be guilty of this offence even if he believed that the female was 16 or older. However, where the female is between 14 and 16, the male isn't guilty unless it can be proved that he was more to blame than the female.

The maximum penalty for having intercourse with a female between 14 and 16 is five years in prison. If the female is under 14 the maximum is life imprisonment.

It is also an indictable offence for a male over the age of 18 to seduce a female of previously chaste character who is between 16 and 18. This is an indictable offence carrying a maximum penalty of imprisonment for two years.

It is a defence to prove that the female was not of previously chaste character; however, she must have lost her chastity through some other agent than the accused.

The Criminal Code provides that, in the case of sexual intercourse with a female between 14 and 16 and seducing a female between 16 and 18, evidence that the accused person had sexual intercourse with the female prior to the date of the alleged offence is not a defence.

Seduce is defined as "to induce to surrender chastity, to lead away or astray." Seduction is defined in *Black's Law Dictionary* as "the act of seducing. Act of man enticing woman to have unlawful intercourse with him by means of persuasion, solicitation, promises, bribes, or other means without employment of force."

It is also an offence for a male over 21 years of age to seduce an unmarried female of previously chaste character under a promise of marriage if the female is under 21 years of age. Once again this is an indictable offence carrying a maximum jail term of two years.

b. PROSTITUTION

Prostitution refers to the selling of the services of oneself or another for the purpose of sexual intercourse. It means to sell one's artistic or moral integrity for a low or unworthy purpose or to be given over to base purposes. The noun "prostitute" refers to a person who engages in promiscuous sexual intercourse for pay.

Prostitution in itself is not illegal in Canada. However, houses of prostitution, called common bawdy houses, are unlawful, and it is unlawful to be an inmate of a bawdy house.

Street prostitution, strictly speaking, is not illegal, but it is illegal to communicate with a person in a public place for the purpose of prostitution. Soliciting is a summary offence punishable by six months in jail, or a fine of $2 000, or both.

The "communicating for the purpose" charge relating to prostitution is based on a public policy desire to keep the streets orderly. Before the soliciting law, known prostitutes could be challenged under the vagrancy "C" — section of the Criminal code, which has now been repealed.

Under the new section, a person who, in a public place or in a place open to public view, stops or attempts to stop any motor vehicle or any pedestrian, or in any manner communicates or attempts to communicate with any person for the purpose of engaging in prostitution or of obtaining the sexual services of a prostitute, may be charged with communicating for the purpose.

Since police must have actual evidence of communicating for the purpose, they may arrange a "sting" operation with an undercover officer body wired to record the conversation, which can then be replayed in court to prove that the communication was for the purpose of prostitution.

Men or women can be charged with communicating for the purposes of prostitution. The law is quite clear that both the customer and the prostitute can be charged, and a customer arrested in a house of prostitution or bawdy house can be charged as a found-in (See chapter 9).

In addition, a person of either sex can be charged with the offence of living off the avails of prostitution (loosely referred to as pimping). It is an indictable offence punishable by up to 10 years in prison to procure, attempt to procure, or solicit a female person to have illicit sexual intercourse with another person.

The definition of procuring also includes the acts of inveigling or enticing a female person who is not a prostitute to a common bawdy house for the purpose of illicit sexual intercourse or prostitution.

c. ABORTION

In the well-publicized Morgentaler case in the Supreme Court of Canada, the Criminal Code provisions relating to abortion were struck down as being unconstitutional. The previous requirement that an abortion could be lawful in Canada only if performed by a qualified medical practitioner who, in good faith, procured the miscarriage of a female in an accredited or approved hospital, no longer applies. Nor is it now necessary to have approval of the majority of a therapeutic abortion committee prior to the procedure being carried out.

Parliament has not yet passed any new laws on abortion. This subject is one of great controversy at the moment, with the pro-life movement demanding some kind of limit on this procedure, and the pro-choice faction demanding that no restraints be imposed by Parliament.

In the meantime, various provincial governments have moved to impose their own restrictions. In some cases, they have refused to pay for the abortion procedure via the usual medical services plan operating in the province. There has been much public outcry over this kind of restriction, and it is doubtful whether any such measures would survive a court challenge.

d. VENEREAL DISEASES

Although it is no longer a Criminal Code offence to knowingly communicate a venereal disease to another person, there are such offences under provincial legislation. It remains a Criminal Code offence to advertise something to be used as a method of restoring sexual virility or curing venereal disease or diseases of the generative organs. This offence may be proceeded with summarily or by indictment.

e. NUDITY

It is illegal to be nude in a public place or on private property if you are in public view. The word nude is defined in the Criminal Code as being "so clad as to offend against public decency or order."

The law doesn't give any standard of public decency or suggest what offends public order. Nudity is a summary offence and the consent of the provincial Attorney General must be obtained before any prosecution can be started.

f. INDECENT ACT OR PERFORMANCE

Committing an indecent act in a public place in the presence of one or more persons, or in any place with intent to insult or offend anyone, is a summary offence.

The Criminal Code defines a public place as "any place to which the public has access as of right or by invitation, express or implied." The term indecent act is not defined, although the general definitions of the term include the following: "something offensive to common propriety, offending against modesty or delicacy, grossly vulgar or obscene or lewd or unseemly or unbecoming or indecorous, unfit to be seen or heard."

It is also an offence for people operating a theatre to present or allow to be presented an immoral, indecent, or obscene performance, entertainment, or representation. In addition, it is an offence for any actor or performer to take part in an immoral, indecent, or obscene performance, entertainment, or representation in a theatre.

It is no defence that such persons did not charge admission to the performance. The penalties for this offence are six months' imprisonment, a $2 000 fine, or both if proceeded with summarily, which is usual, or a maximum of up to two years in jail if the Crown proceeded by indictment.

A detailed discussion of the law on obscenity is beyond the scope of this book; however, the topic is covered briefly in chapter 9, dealing with search and seizure in obscenity cases.

g. GROSS INDECENCY

It is illegal to commit an act of gross indecency with another person. The offence of gross indecency is indictable and carries a maximum penalty of imprisonment for five years or a fine or both. The term gross indecency is not defined by the Criminal Code. There is some uncertainty as to what sexual behavior might violate the law.

The law states that a husband and wife, or two people over 21 years of age, may perform any sexual act in private if both consent. However, such an act is not considered to be private if more than two persons are present to take part in the act, or if it is carried on in a public place.

23
BAIL: RELEASE BY POLICE OFFICERS

This chapter and the next few chapters deal with the position of the person who has been charged with an offence and has been arrested.

The word bail has traditionally been used when a person is released from custody pending trial. The word itself may be going out of use, as the Criminal Code now refers to the act of obtaining bail from a court as "judicial interim release," rather than bail. However, the Constitution refers to bail in Section 11(e) of the Charter, which provides a constitutional right of a person charged with an offence "not to be denied bail without just cause."

Also for many of the less serious offences it is not necessary for police to actually arrest you in order to lay a criminal charge. In these cases, the attending constable can issue an appearance notice, requiring an appearance for fingerprinting and photographing in the case of an indictable offence.

An attending officer who makes an arrest can later change his or her mind and release you on an appearance notice, or release you with the intention of later arranging for the issuance of a summons.

a. APPEARANCE NOTICE ISSUED BY ATTENDING OFFICER

The Criminal Code directs the attending police officer to issue an appearance notice, rather than make an arrest, to persons charged with minor offences. This includes the following offences:

(a) Summary offences, of which causing a disturbance and unlawful assembly are examples

(b) Offences which may be summary or indictable, which include the following:
   (i) Impaired driving offences
   (ii) Charges of simple possession of a drug
   (iii) Charges of theft, possession, false pretenses, or fraud, where the value of the property is less than $1 000
   (iv) Assault
   (v) Possession of restricted or prohibited weapons
   (vi) Assaulting or obstructing a police officer
(c) Indictable offences, which must be tried before a magistrate or provincial court judge, including the following:
   (i) Betting, gaming, bookmaking, and lottery charges
   (ii) Cheating at play
   (iii) Offences in relation to a common bawdy house, that is, being a keeper, inmate, found-in, or lessor of a bawdy house
   (iv) Fraud in relation to transportation fares and tickets

However, the police officer may make an arrest when considered necessary to —

(a) establish the identity of the accused,

(b) secure or preserve evidence of or relating to the offence,

(c) prevent the continuation or repetition of the offence or the commission of another offence,

(d) or where the officer has grounds to believe that the person may fail to attend court if not arrested.

An appearance notice will require a court appearance to set a trial date and may also require an appearance for fingerprinting or photographing in the case of an indictable offence.

b. RELEASE AFTER ARREST

The attending officer still has the authority to release an accused person after making an arrest. At this stage, the officer may issue an appearance notice, or may release you with the intention of compelling your appearance by a summons.

The power to release after an arrest applies to the same offences mentioned above and the same considerations, such as the need to establish the identity of the accused, and so on, also apply.

c. RELEASE BY OFFICER-IN-CHARGE

The commanding officer-in-charge of the police shift has wider powers than an arresting officer to release an accused person. In addition to those cases in which the attending officer may release by appearance notice or summons, the officer-in-charge can also release a person charged with an indictable offence carrying a maximum penalty of five years or less.

The officer-in-charge also has greater flexibility in the type of release that he or she may grant, and may release a person in any of the following ways:

(a) Unconditionally, with the intention of compelling appearance by way of summons

(b) By promise to appear

(c) On a recognizance without sureties (these terms are defined in the next chapter), and without deposit

(d) In the case of non-residents, on cash bail not exceeding $500, with deposit if the officer wishes

The officer-in-charge also has power to release a person arrested with a warrant except a person arrested on the basis of an out-of-province warrant.

In more serious cases, such as where the accused has a criminal record, police are not likely to permit a release and will turn the case over to a justice of the peace, who may order release or may wait for the case to go before a provincial court judge.

Anyone who is charged with an offence carrying a maximum penalty of five years or more must, of course, appear before a justice or provincial court judge.

The justice of the peace will not deal with serious cases, which often means that the accused will remain in jail overnight or, if the arrest occurred on a Saturday, there may not be a court appearance until Monday morning.

d. RIGHT TO APPEAR BEFORE A JUSTICE OR JUDGE

Any person in custody on a criminal offence has a right to appear before a justice of the peace, a magistrate, or provincial court judge within 24 hours or as soon as possible after one is available.

The issue of bail will be dealt with at this time, although the prosecutor or the accused can apply to adjourn the bail application for a period of up to three days, but no more, except with the consent of the accused.

24
HOW AND WHEN DO YOU GET BAIL?

a. YOUR RIGHT TO A BAIL HEARING

To recap, if the police do not release you after an arrest, you have the right to appear before a justice, magistrate, or provincial judge within 24 hours, or as soon as possible, to have bail set.

It is, of course, advisable to have a lawyer make the bail application. In most urban centres, legal aid lawyers or public defenders are available to speak for you if you cannot afford your own lawyer.

Where no form of legal aid is available, request the court to appoint a lawyer for you.

b. REASONABLE BAIL

The Charter of Rights and Freedoms provides a constitutional guarantee of the right to have reasonable bail. This right cannot be denied without just cause. Unfortunately, neither the Constitution nor the Bill of Rights, which contains a similar guarantee, resolves the question of what reasonable bail is, or what just cause for denying bail is.

The Constitution also guarantees that a person charged with a criminal offence has the right to be presumed innocent until proven guilty, according to law, in a fair and public hearing. In theory, then, bail should not be denied in many cases.

c. BAIL REFORM ACT AND AMENDMENTS

The Bail Reform Act of 1972 was a fairly liberal bill, greatly benefiting accused people and compelling prosecutors to show why an accused person should not be released on bail.

If the prosecutors failed to show reasons why the accused should not be released on bail, then release on an undertaking to appear for trial would be automatic.

If the prosecutor was able to show reason, then release could be on an undertaking with conditions or on a recognizance. A cash deposit was required if the accused was a non-resident.

However, Parliament has since taken a more conservative position. Now, in many cases, the pressure to show cause is on the accused rather than the prosecutor. However, in most straightforward cases the prosecutor must still show cause for detention.

d. CASES WHERE PROSECUTOR MUST SHOW CAUSE

An accused person will normally be released when he or she appears before a justice, magistrate, or provincial judge on one of the following offences:

(a) Simple possession of a drug

(b) Common assault

(c) Causing a disturbance

(d) Unlawful assembly

(e) Drinking and driving offences (including impaired driving, with more than 80 milligrams of alcohol per 100 millilitres of blood)

(f) Refusal to take a breathalyzer test

(g) Soliciting

(h) Theft (including shoplifting)

(i) Possession under $1 000

(j) False pretenses under $1 000

(k) Fraud where the property is valued at less than $1 000

(l) Mischief or wilful damage

In all these cases, the prosecutor is required to show why you should not be released. The prosecutor must show one of the following things:

(a) That you will not show up for court when required

(b) That your detention is necessary in the public interest or for the protection or safety of the public, having regard to any "substantial likelihood" that you will, if released, commit a further criminal offence or interfere with the administration of justice

e. NON-RESIDENTS

Beyond the simple general rule, all sorts of exceptions and complications could occur. For example, if you are a non-resident, the prosecutor will have less difficulty showing why you should not be released on a simple undertaking. In this situation, the judge can release you on a cash bail recognizance, requiring you to deposit the stated sum.

f. BAIL WITH CONDITIONS

If the charge involves violence against another person and the judge feels there is a danger to the witnesses, he may release you on an undertaking or recognizance with conditions (such as requiring that you have no contact with the victim or other witnesses).

If you have a previous conviction for failing to appear in court, the judge may require that you report to the police once a week or that you deposit your passport. If you have a record for similar offences, the judge may impose a bail with conditions or deny bail.

g. REMAND FOR OBSERVATION

If there are signs that you are mentally ill, the judge can, with medical evidence or on the basis of his or her own opinion (where medical evidence is not available), remand you for observation for 30 days. If the judge has medical evidence justifying his or her opinion that you are mentally ill, you can be remanded for psychological assessment for a period of 30 to 60 days.

h. BAIL WITH AGREEMENT OF PROSECUTOR

If the prosecutor agrees, you can be released on your own recognizance, without sureties, in any amount and with any conditions as the judge directs. The judge could direct a deposit of cash or other valuables. Conditions that can be ordered include the following:

(a) Reporting to police at certain times

(b) Remaining in the territory of the court

(c) Notifying police of any change in address or employment

(d) Not communicating with any witness or other person

(e) Depositing your passport

(f) Other reasonable conditions (these may include abstention from consumption of alcohol or drugs, if there is evidence that drugs or alcohol may be involved in the alleged offence)

i. PROCEDURE AT A BAIL HEARING

You are entitled to an order that the evidence and submissions at the bail hearing not be published or broadcast until after the case has ended.

The prosecutor is entitled to prove that you have a criminal record, that you are awaiting trial on other charges, or that you have previously failed to appear.

The Crown can also refer to the circumstances of the offence in order to show the probability of conviction. This seems contrary to the constitutional right to be presumed innocent, and is an issue that will be considered by the courts in due course.

j. CASH BAIL, SURETY, AND RECOGNIZANCE

A word must be said here about sureties, recognizances, and cash bails. Normally, a cash bail will not be required unless the accused does not reside within 100 miles of the courthouse. Cash bail means that cash must actually be deposited.

A recognizance is an acknowledgment of the accused of the legal obligation to appear in court when required and a pledge to be legally responsible for the stated sum in the recognizance if he or she fails to appear.

An "Own Recognizance" ("OR") bail simply means that the accused is let out on his or her own signature, without sureties and without a deposit of money.

A surety is a person other than the accused, possibly a friend or relative, who signs a recognizance to obtain the release of the accused on bail. The courts generally require sureties in more serious cases.

Traditionally, the courts have felt that the surety, who stands to lose money if the accused fails to appear for trial, will guarantee the presence or return of the accused for court.

Unless the bail order is formally changed, or a warrant is issued for the accused, a recognizance of bail continues until acquittal or sentence. The accused must make required court appearances.

k. ILLEGAL TO INDEMNIFY BONDSMEN

In Canada, there are no professional bondsmen. It is illegal for any accused person or anyone else to indemnify or agree to indemnify a surety in whole or in part. This would include any payment of a fee to a person for agreeing to be a surety or provide money for cash bail.

Any surety who agrees to accept a fee or any form of indemnification also commits an illegal act. These offences are described as "obstructing justice," and are indictable, carrying a maximum penalty of two years or a summary conviction offence.

Our system is in contrast to the United States system in this regard where professional bondsmen are fairly common. In Canada, a person or group can assist in putting up bail, provided no fee is taken for doing this.

The theory behind the Canadian law seems to be that the surety takes the risk of losing the bail if the accused fails to turn up for court. Generally, where a surety is required, the accused must rely on friends or other persons to take a risk for him or her.

l. CONSEQUENCES OF A FAILURE TO APPEAR

If you fail to appear, the following things may occur:

(a) A warrant will be issued for your arrest.

(b) You will also be charged with failing to appear.

(c) The bail can be *estreated*, or forfeited to the Crown.

If the bail is forfeited, a judge will set a date for an application for forfeiture. The clerk of the court will notify the accused, if he or she can be found, and surety or sureties, and request them to appear to show why the recognizance should not be forfeited.

The surety will have an opportunity to be heard, and the judge has complete discretion to grant or refuse the prosecutor's application for forfeiture. If forfeiture is ordered, the principal and sureties become judgment debtors of the Crown. A sheriff can ultimately seize property of the sureties to satisfy the amount owed to the Crown.

If the sheriff is unable to find sufficient goods, there could be a warrant of committal. That is, there is potentially a danger that the surety could be given a short jail term or at least committed to custody until the amount is paid.

m. TURNING IN THE ACCUSED

A surety is entitled to turn the accused in to the court and ask to be relieved from the obligation of the recognizance. If the accused cannot be found, the surety can apply in writing to be relieved of the obligation, in which case the accused will be arrested on a warrant.

It is obviously very important, if you are asking someone to give bail for you, to be diligent about turning up for court. (Similarly, if you are asked to be a surety, make sure your friend turns up!)

n. ARREST IN ANOTHER PROVINCE

Police have power to arrest a person charged with an indictable offence in a province other than the province where the offence occurred.

They also have the power to arrest a person on a warrant for an offence in another province, provided that a local justice has authorized execution of the warrant within his or her jurisdiction.

A person arrested without warrant for an indictable offence alleged to have been committed in another province must be brought before a justice within 24 hours. The justice must decide if there are reasonable and probable grounds to believe that the person arrested is the person alleged to have committed the offence.

If the judge is not satisfied that there are reasonable and probable grounds to believe that the person arrested is the person who committed the offence, he or she will release the person.

If reasonable and probable grounds are found, the judge can have the accused held in custody to await a warrant for arrest. However, if no warrant is signed within six days, the person is entitled to be released.

25
DENIAL OF BAIL AND OTHER DIFFICULTIES

a. DENIAL OF BAIL

In some situations, the judge may order that the accused be detained in custody until the trial. This will normally arise if the charge is very serious and the judge believes, on the basis of the prosecutor's submissions, that there is a danger the accused will abscond if released on bail.

A judge may also refuse bail if the accused appears to be a bad risk because of previous convictions for failing to appear in court when required.

If the accused is a non-resident with no reason to remain in the jurisdiction once released, the judge may deny bail.

The judge will also deny bail if the prosecutor shows that the accused is likely to commit further offences or endanger the witnesses if released on bail.

b. APPEAL FROM DETENTION ORDER

You have the right to appeal against a detention order to the county or district court or a supreme or superior court for a review of the bail order.

Generally speaking, the whole question of bail may be re-examined by a higher court judge to find out if the magistrate or provincial court judge or justice has made an error in detaining you in custody. The prosecutor is also entitled to an appeal from a bail order granting release.

c. CASES WHERE ACCUSED MUST SHOW CAUSE

The cases where you must show why you should be granted bail are as follows:

(a) Where you have committed an indictable offence while already on bail for another indictable offence

(b) Where you are a non-resident charged with an indictable offence

(c) Where you are charged with failing to appear for court, or breach of a bail order, while on bail for any other offence

(d) Where you are charged with trafficking, possession for the purpose of trafficking, importing, or exporting a narcotic under Sections 4 or 5 of the Narcotic Control Act, or with conspiracy to commit any such offence

In all these cases, the burden is on the defence to show why you should be released on bail. If this is done to the satisfaction of the judge or magistrate, you are entitled to be released.

d. THE MOST SERIOUS CASES

In all the most serious offences, such as first or second degree murder, treason, intimidating Parliament, sabotage, mutiny, hijacking, or endangering an aircraft in flight, the justice, magistrate, or judge will make a detention order, and the bail application will proceed before a judge of the superior court.

In the absence of unusual circumstances, and where the prosecutor fails to show that detention in custody is justified, the accused is entitled to be released on bail.

However, in the following circumstances, the defence must prove that release is justified.

(a) You committed an offence while on bail for another indictable offence.

(b) You are a non-resident.

(c) You are charged with an offence, such as skipping bail, committed while awaiting trial for one of these serious offences.

(d) You are charged with murder or conspiring to commit murder.

Appeal from a bail order in these more serious matters lies with the court of appeal.

e. RIGHT TO TRIAL WITHIN A REASONABLE TIME

Any person charged with an offence in Canada has a constitutional right to be tried within a reasonable time. While the constitution does not further define what a reasonable time is, the courts have indicated the various factors that are to be considered in terms of computing that time.

Those factors include whether the delay is due to actions of the defence or the prosecution, or whether it may be as a result of the court system, and whether the defence has agreed to the delay or asserted the right to be tried within a reasonable time.

An accused person whose right to trial within a reasonable time has been denied by undue delay has as a minimum remedy the right under Section 24(1) to a stay or termination of the court proceedings against him.

This is not expressed in the Constitution, but has been decided by the Supreme Court of Canada to be the appropriate remedy. The court has also indicated that in other situations additional remedies, such as damages, may be appropriate.

f. DELAY OF TRIAL IN CASES OF DETENTION

If a detention order is made and an appeal, if taken, is unsuccessful, you may remain in custody until your trial. However, if the trial, in the case of an indictable offence, has not proceeded within 90 days from the date of your arrest, you have the right to a further review of your detention. This is an absolute statutory right. The judge hearing this review can decide to release you or make an order that the trial be set for an earlier date.

In summary matters, you have the right to have your detention reviewed if the trial has not proceeded within 30 days from the date of arrest. Again, the judge will either release you or order that the trial be expedited.

g. PROPOSED CRIMINAL CODE CHANGES

The federal government has been considering legislation in Parliament that would require criminal trials to begin within six months after the accused's first court appearance. Where there is a right to a preliminary hearing on an indictable offence, the preliminary hearing would be required to commence within six months, and the trial must start within six months after the date that the accused is committed to stand trial.

Where these time limits are not met, the charge would be dismissed for want of prosecution, unless the judge was satisfied that it would be in the interests of justice to allow an extension of time. These proposals would be important guidelines for the courts in applying the constitutional right to trial within a reasonable time.

h. REMANDS

Following the bail hearing and the setting of a date for the trial or preliminary hearing, appearances will be required every eight days. You may consent to waive these whether or not you are in custody. If you are concerned that the authorities may forget about you, you may wish to make the eight-day appearances. You may also air any questions, difficulties, or complaints to the judge during these remands.

If you are on bail, you and your sureties, if any, can appear, and agree to the case going directly to the trial date without the necessary interim remands.

i. VIOLATION OF BAIL

If a constable or judge learns that you are planning to violate a condition of your bail order or abscond, or commit another offence, you can be arrested with or without a warrant. Obviously, it will be more difficult to be released again. It is very important to abide completely by the bail order and the conditions to it.

Once the trial begins, the presiding judge has an absolute discretion in the matter of whether to continue bail. However, bail will normally continue until the time of verdict.

j. THE ACCUSED IN CUSTODY

The problem with an accused person who is denied bail is magnified by several factors. First of all, such a person is doing what is called "dead time." That is, the accused is, in effect, serving time before the trial. Dead time must be considered by the trial judge in sentencing the accused, but the parole board is required to take it into account only in murder cases.

In addition, communication with the outside world is difficult. Most remand units lack pre-trial services, such as use of telephones, proper visiting facilities, libraries, and so forth.

There is also a lack of privacy, as prison authorities can be expected to monitor incoming and outgoing mail to determine whether contraband is being passed.

There is also the risk that informers or undercover officers may be planted in the prison to induce statements or provide an opportunity for a confession.

26
BEFORE THE TRIAL

a. THE WISDOM OF HAVING A LAWYER

In preparing for your trial, you should first obtain the services of a lawyer. There is an old saying: "a lawyer who acts for himself has a fool for a client." In lawyer circles, this refers to the fact that it is usually embarrassing and detrimental to attempt to defend yourself in a criminal court.

There are many reasons for this, and it will suffice to mention some of the obvious ones. Although everyone is presumed innocent, it is obvious to judges and prosecutors that an accused person has a self-interest in the case. Generally, it is far better in terms of the credibility of your case to have representations made by a lawyer, rather than yourself. In cross-examining, for example, if you are representing yourself you will almost invariably betray more than you intend in attempting to question witnesses.

The foregoing considerations are entirely apart from the question of whether a lay person will be familiar with court procedures, with defences that may be available, with advantages that might be gained from actions of the prosecution, with potential consequences of the case, and so on.

Even where you are charged with a summary offence and intend to plead guilty to it, it is still a good rule of thumb to speak with a lawyer before appearing in court. Judges are sympathetic to this and will be willing to grant one or two adjournments in order to give you this opportunity. The reason is that there may sometimes be defences to charges that an accused person will not have considered. Indeed, the consequences of the offence, such as suspension of driver's licence following an impaired driving conviction, may not have been considered.

b. LEGAL FEES

There is considerable variability in fees charged by lawyers. Generally, fees in a criminal case will be based on the time required for preparation, the length, and the complexity of the case; they will also be based on the experience and skill of the lawyer. Criminal lawyers normally require payment in full before the trial.

c. LEGAL AID

Previous chapters have dealt with the right to counsel which is a constitutional right guaranteed in the Charter. In Canada, everyone has the right to legal counsel on a criminal charge. There may be some restriction as to summary offences in some provinces.

If you can't afford a lawyer, apply for legal aid. To find out about legal aid, contact the nearest Salvation Army post, the John Howard or Elizabeth Fry Societies, the local Bar Association or Law Society office, or the local office of the Canadian Bar Association, or ask the judge before whom you appear about legal aid. If you cannot get legal aid and you cannot afford a lawyer, ask the judge for a court-appointed lawyer.

d. THE TRIAL DATE

In Canada, there is no guarantee of an early trial date. However, Section 11(b) of the Charter gives the right to be tried within a reasonable time. Undue delay by the prosecution in bringing the case to trial may result in dismissal of the charges.

If, for whatever reason, you want an early trial, you must bring it to the attention of the court at the time a trial date is being set.

However, in addition to the constitutional right to be tried within a reasonable time, there are also Criminal Code provisions allowing a judge to expedite the trial where the accused is in custody and the trial has been delayed. As we have already seen, if you are still in custody 30 days after your first court appearance on a summary offence, or 90 days after the date of the first court offence on an indictable offence, your custodians or the jailer must apply to a judge for a hearing to determine whether you should be released.

In this hearing, the judge must consider whether the delay was caused by the accused or the prosecutor, and whether the further detention of the accused is justified. The judge may also give directions for expediting the trial.

e. RIGHT TO BE INFORMED WITHOUT UNREASONABLE DELAY

Section 11(a) of the Charter of Rights and Freedoms provides that an accused person has the right to be informed without unreasonable delay of the specific offence. This presumably means within 24 hours after the time of arrest.

An accused person can obtain a copy of the information containing the charge from the office of the court clerk. After a preliminary hearing, an accused person is entitled to inspect the indictment (a name applied to the document containing the charge when it is in county or superior court), his or her own statement (if any), the evidence that has been taken under oath at the preliminary hearing, and any exhibits which were filed.

On payment of a reasonable fee, the accused is entitled to a copy of the evidence, his or her own statement (if any), and a copy of the indictment. You are not entitled to an adjournment of your trial to obtain these copies unless you can show that failure to obtain them prior to trial was not due to lack of diligence on your part.

f. PARTICULARS

The lawyer for an accused person is entitled to apply for particulars of the allegations against the accused.

In provincial court matters, or before a preliminary hearing, defence lawyers normally obtain what are referred to as "informal particulars" by telephone or by informal written request to the prosecutor.

These informal particulars are not binding on the Crown counsel, but they are generally a summary of the minutes of evidence that the Crown counsel expects the witnesses to give at trial or preliminary hearing. In minor cases they are generally sufficient to inform you as to the specific allegations against you.

For example, on an impaired driving case these informal particulars will describe the driving that attracted police attention, the behavior the police claim was consistent with impairment by alcohol, details of what occurred at the time of breath test, any statements made to the police, and so on.

To take another example, in a case where an accused has been arrested with other persons in a house in which narcotics have been found, informal particulars will describe the amounts and locations of drugs that were found, give a description of the packaging of the drugs, describe actions of the suspects at the time of the search that might be relevant, and give statements that were made.

A general caution is in order in cases where informal particulars are sought. As mentioned above, they are not binding on the Crown, nor are they necessarily complete. For example, it is not uncommon to find informal particulars omitting reference to a statement attributable to an accused and led in evidence at the trial.

In addition, if the facts at trial evolve differently than the informal particulars, there is no recourse. In some cases, such problems can be avoided by an application for formal particulars.

g. APPLICATION FOR FORMAL PARTICULARS

An application for formal particulars can be made before a trial or any time during the trial. The judge will order particulars to be provided if he or she feels it is necessary for a fair trial.

Generally, particulars can be anything describing the means by which an offence is alleged to have been committed, or describing in more detail a person, place, or thing that is referred to in a charge, or any other form of particulars that may be necessary in the particular case for a fair trial.

Formal particulars must be proved by the Crown, and the trial proceeds as if the indictment had been amended to include the particulars.

h. ARRAIGNMENT

The term "arraignment" means appearing before the trial judge and pleading to the charge. If you are charged with an indictable offence, you may have an option to be tried by magistrate, higher court judge, or judge and jury.

If you choose trial by higher court judge and jury, the magistrate will hold a preliminary hearing. You will be brought to the bar to plead, or be arraigned, in the higher court.

i. RIGHT TO A JURY TRIAL

Every person charged with an offence carrying a maximum punishment of five years or more is entitled "to the benefit of trial by jury." This means that most persons charged with indictable offences will have the right to choose to be tried by a judge and a jury.

On most offences where a jury trial is available, when the accused appears before the magistrate or provincial court judge for a preliminary hearing before being called upon to plead, the accused will be asked to elect whether to be tried by a judge and jury, judge without jury, or magistrate without jury.

Where the accused chooses a magistrate without a jury, the trial will proceed before the magistrate or provincial court judge. If the accused chooses a judge and jury or judge without jury, the magistrate has jurisdiction only to hold a preliminary inquiry and to decide if there is enough evidence for a trial.

In such cases, the trial will take place later before a judge or judge and jury in the county or district or superior court of the province, depending on the choice and depending on the province. For example, in Ontario, judge and jury trials are held in superior court or in county or district court. This is also true for British Columbia, Newfoundland, and

Manitoba. In Saskatchewan and Alberta, these cases are heard only in superior court, and in Prince Edward Island, the Yukon Territory and the Northwest Territories such cases are heard in Supreme Court. In Quebec, they are heard before a judge of the sessions of the peace or a judge of the provincial court; in New Brunswick, before a judge of the Court of Queen's Bench. In Nova Scotia, there is no entitlement to have a trial before a superior court judge, and such cases are heard before the county court.

There are a few indictable offences that must be tried by a magistrate or provincial court judge and on which an accused person does not have the right to a jury trial. Common offences that fall within this rule are those involving gaming, gambling, betting, lotteries, and bookmaking; being the keeper or inmate, found-in or lessor of a bawdy house; driving while under suspension; theft, possession, false pretenses, or fraud in all cases where the value of the subject matter is under $1 000.

Certain major offences that formerly required trial by jury (rape, attempted rape, criminal negligence causing death, and manslaughter) are now electable. In addition, all summary offences, such as soliciting, causing a disturbance and so on, may be tried only before a magistrate or provincial court judge. In these cases there is no right of choice and no right to a preliminary hearing.

Your choice, or election, and plea may be very important to your defence. You should discuss these matters with your lawyer before committing yourself to a course of action. If the court asks you to elect or plead before you have counsel or before you have discussed this with your lawyer, you want to ask for a week's adjournment to obtain counsel or discuss the matter with counsel.

There are many cases in which it is useful to have a preliminary hearing to learn something more of the Crown's allegations against you.

j. PRELIMINARY HEARINGS

In a preliminary hearing, the prosecutor is required to produce witnesses to give evidence under oath to support the allegations against you. Your lawyer has the right to cross-examine the Crown witnesses.

At the end of the prosecutor's evidence, you have the right to call witnesses or to make a statement to the court. You are not required to do either of these things.

If you make any statement, it will be taken down by the court reporter and can be used as evidence against you later at the trial.

The defence normally does not lead evidence at a preliminary hearing, from the accused or any defence witnesses. At the end of the inquiry, if the evidence is weak, your lawyer may make a motion for discharge, arguing that on the basis of the evidence there is an insufficient case to commit you for trial.

The judge will decide whether there is evidence on which a judge or jury could find you guilty of the offence charged; sometimes the test is referred to as one of "probable guilt." The point is that the prosecutor is not required to prove the case beyond a reasonable doubt at a preliminary hearing.

Bail normally continues through to the end of the trial or sentence. However, if there are changed circumstances, such as new charges, evidence that you are about to abscond, or if you threaten a witness, bail can be revoked.

In high court, arraignment or plea occurs on the day of the trial. If there is a jury, your arraignment occurs in the presence of the jury.

k. PROPOSAL FOR PRE-TRIAL CONFERENCES

There has been a proposed legislative amendment that would allow judges to order pre-trial conferences. These would be conducted in the presence of counsel for the Crown and the accused and would be presided over by the judge. Informal pre-trial conferences in the past have been used to find ways of reducing the length of trial.

Under the proposed legislation, the court may order a pre-trial conference to consider matters that will "promote a fair and expeditious hearing."

This proposal is designed to give judges the opportunity to cut down the time required for basically non-contentious proceedings and shorten trials.

1. PLEA BARGAINING

Plea bargaining refers to the situation where the prosecutor compromises with the defence lawyer to arrange the settlement of one or more charges against you. It may involve agreement to drop some charges in return for a plea of guilty to one or others. It may also involve the prosecutor agreeing to take a certain position in sentencing, such as not asking for a jail term.

For example, where you are charged with possession of marijuana for the purpose of trafficking, the prosecutor may agree to reduce the charge to one of simple possession in return for a guilty plea. From the point of view of both defence lawyer and client, this will frequently be an attractive offer as it will place the case into a much lower range of potential penalty. If this is done, the prosecutor would stay the proceedings, amend or withdraw the charge of possession for the purpose of trafficking, and proceed on a new or amended charge of simple possession to which you would plead guilty.

A word of caution: Plea bargaining occurs all the time; it is obviously an efficient manner in which a prosecutor can deal with a large number of charges against one person, reduce the consumption of court time if there is a backlog of cases, or avoid the situation where a number of police officers are tied up for a lengthy period on one case and so on. It can obviously be beneficial to the accused.

Nevertheless, you should bear in mind that it is unwise to consider any form of plea bargaining with police on the basis of a misconception that the police have the right to bind the prosecutor or the judge. The judge is not involved in plea bargaining in Canada and has no obligation to go along with any plans that the police or the prosecutor may have for an accused person. In fact, it is open for the judge to take a different tack completely. That is not to say that judges do not frequently go along with the recommendations of prosecutors. They certainly do, but it is not something that can be counted on absolutely. Your lawyer will be able to give you guidance in this regard.

m. STAY OF PROCEEDINGS

In summary or indictable offences, the prosecutor may decide at any time to stay the proceedings in a case. A stay of proceedings is exactly what it says — a stop in the proceedings. They can be started again.

In fact, proceedings are usually stayed when there is no evidence on which to proceed, or as a result of a plea bargain, or for some reason of fairness or expediency. This means that cases in which there has been a stay of proceedings are seldom heard from again. However, it should be perfectly clear that a stay of proceedings is not the same thing as being acquitted of a charge.

The other aspect of a stay of proceedings is that it has nothing to do with the judge, but is something that can be arbitrarily done by a prosecutor. The prosecutor is entitled to stay the proceedings in any case.

This means that the accused has no right to ultimately be proven innocent, and it also means that the judge has no power to deal further with the matter unless some other person proceeds with a private prosecution.

A charge that has been stayed and is not re-activated within one year is deemed never to have been laid. In the case of summary offences where the limitation period for beginning proceedings is six months, a charge that is stayed must be re-started within that six-month period or it can never be started again. For other summary offences the charge must be proceeded with within one year after a stay of proceedings.

For indictable offences, a charge which has been the subject of a stay of proceedings can be re-started within one year upon the Crown counsel giving notice to the court clerk. However, for most indictable offences in Canada there is no time limitation within which the Crown must proceed. This means that it will usually be within the power of the Crown to start proceedings afresh by laying a new information or preferring an indictment.

n. MOTIONS TO QUASH

The law requires that the charge against an accused person must be worded in such a way as to give you notice of the offence with which you are charged.

Each charge must contain sufficient detail of the circumstances of the alleged offence to give you "reasonable information" about the act or omission that is alleged against you and "to identify the transaction referred to." Frequently, lawyers will attach a charge that does not conform with the above requirements, on the basis that it is unclear, vague, or uncertain, that it fails to disclose an offence known to law, that it does not sufficiently identify the transaction, or that it does not give the accused reasonable information with respect to what is alleged.

Defence counsel will argue that the charge is invalid and must be quashed. Crown counsel will frequently argue that the charge is capable of amendment. If the judge quashes the charge, the Crown may proceed again by laying a new charge.

o. MOTION FOR A SEPARATE TRIAL

There are two kinds of motions for a separate trial. A person who is charged together with a number of other people may apply to have a separate trial. It is a general rule that people who are jointly charged with the commission of the same offence or with being engaged in a common enterprise will normally be tried together.

The trial judge always has the discretion to order separate trials if satisfied "that the ends of justice require it." Separate trials have been granted on the following bases:

- (a) In a case where evidence admissible against one accused is not admissible against the others, such as where one of the accused has made a confession which is evidence against him but not against the others

(b) In a case where one accused wishes to call a co-accused as a witness, because the co-accused as witness would not be entitled to the protection against self-incrimination under the Canada Evidence Act

(c) In a case where an important part of the defence of one accused consists of an attack upon the other accused

It is important to realize that a separate trial will not be granted in every instance where one of the above applies.

An application for a separate trial is generally made to the trial judge before or at the beginning of the trial. A judge will be more inclined to grant it in the case of a jury trial where he or she feels prejudice may result to the accused.

You may be tried on several charges at the same time, but you are entitled to apply for a separate trial on one or more of the charges. If the court is satisfied that justice requires it, it may order that you be tried separately on one or more of the counts.

In addition, where a count charges several different matters that are stated in the alternative, you are entitled to apply to the court to amend or divide that count into two or more counts.

27
THE COURSE OF THE TRIAL

Proceedings at Canadian criminal trials tend to be quite formal in nature. The trial always begins with your arraignment and your plea to the charge.

If it is a jury trial, you are formally placed in the charge of the jury, and the jury will be asked to select a foreman before the taking of evidence begins. Crown counsel is entitled to make an opening statement to the court. This statement is not evidence but is merely a summary of the evidence that the Crown expects the witnesses to give.

The Crown witnesses are then called one by one, their evidence led "in chief" by Crown counsel, who is not entitled to ask leading questions, and then cross-examined by defence counsel.

At the end of the Crown's case, defence counsel is entitled to make what is referred to as a "no evidence" motion or a motion for directed verdict. This motion is based on an argument that the evidence led by the Crown is not capable of proving the charge against the accused person, or that the jury, if they are properly instructed, could not convict the accused.

This motion is made in the absence of the jury; if the judge agrees with the defence, the jury will be returned to the courtroom and the judge will give them directions to return a verdict of not guilty.

If the judge disagrees with the defence and rules that there is evidence to go to the jury, the defence will be called upon to choose whether to call evidence or not. The defence may call evidence, but is not required to give evidence.

If the defence calls no evidence, then in a trial by judge alone, defence counsel would argue that the charge should be dismissed on the basis that there is no proof beyond a reasonable doubt.

In a jury trial where the defence calls no evidence, Crown counsel is required to address the jury first, with defence counsel going last. The Crown will, of course, argue that the charge is proved beyond a reasonable doubt and the defence will argue that a reasonable doubt exists on the whole of the case.

In a jury trial, where the defence calls evidence, defence counsel has the right to make an opening speech to the jury, but it is only occasionally exercised. Defence witnesses will be called one by one, their evidence led "in chief" by defence counsel, and they will be cross-examined by the Crown. If you are to be called as a witness, you will testify first by answering the questions of your own lawyer, then be cross-examined by Crown counsel. If you have a criminal record, you can be cross-examined upon it for the purpose of questioning your credibility.

Many of the matters dealt with in the previous chapter, such as motions to quash and motions for separate trials, may arise during the course of the trial as well as before the trial. This chapter deals with other procedures that are likely to occur during the course of the trial.

a. ADJOURNMENTS OF THE TRIAL

Circumstances may arise where it is necessary for you to apply for an adjournment of the trial. It may be that your counsel is tied up on another case in a higher court or is ill, or it may be that some important preparations have not been done, or that some critical witness is not available.

A defence counsel who becomes aware that an adjournment will be required on behalf of the accused will normally communicate this to Crown counsel at the earliest possible time so that an appearance can be made before a judge to apply for an adjournment.

The judge hearing an application to adjourn may refuse the adjournment or grant it where the reasons are substantial, it would be unfair to deny the adjournment, and the adjournment would not prejudice the Crown.

Crown counsel may also require an adjournment, due to a missing witness or the unavailability of some piece of documentary evidence on the date set for trial, or for any other reason.

If defence is prepared for trial and you do not wish to have an adjournment, defence may oppose the Crown's request. If the judge agrees with the defence and denies the Crown adjournment, defence may be in a position to move for dismissal of the case for want of prosecution.

In less serious cases, a judge may be persuaded to take this course of action if there is evidence that you or your witnesses are inconvenienced by a further delay of the trial such as by potentially losing employment. However, even in indictable cases, the Crown is required to have satisfactory reasons for the adjournment, and the judge may refuse the application if he or she is not so satisfied.

In some cases, the Crown has taken the approach of entering a stay of proceedings and then re-commencing the charge at a later date, when the case is in order. This practice has sometimes been upheld by the courts, and sometimes the courts have disagreed with it and held that the later proceedings were taken solely to circumvent the earlier ruling of the court and therefore constitute an abuse of process.

b. IS THE ACCUSED REQUIRED TO BE PRESENT THROUGHOUT THE TRIAL?

The Criminal Code guarantees your right as an accused person to be present throughout your trial. However, a defendant charged with a summary offence may appear by counsel or agent unless the court specifically requests the defendant to appear personally.

If it is satisfactory to the prosecutor and to the court, the whole trial and sentencing proceedings can be conducted by the appearance of counsel or an agent and without any appearance by the accused. The Crown may agree to this in cases where there is no issue of identification and in cases where the penalty is certain to be a fine.

In cases where who committed the offence may be an issue, and where in sentencing a jail term may be involved, the Crown would normally not agree to proceeding without your presence, and a judge would likely require you to appear. Failure to appear when required may lead to the issue of a warrant for arrest.

In summary proceedings where you are required by an appearance notice or a summons to appear at the trial and you fail to appear, the court may issue a warrant for your arrest if the prosecutor is able to prove that the summons was served within a reasonable time before the appearance was required.

However, as an alternative, the court may proceed *ex parte* (in the absence of one side) to hear and determine the proceedings in your absence just as if you had actually appeared. This is a comparatively rare procedure, but is available upon the application of Crown counsel, or on the initiative of the court.

In the case of indictable offences, you are required to be present through the whole of your trial except where the court specifically permits you to be away during part of the trial. This procedure is not uncommon in lengthy trials where you have medical appointments or some other good and sufficient cause for being absent.

In addition, an accused who interrupts the proceedings to the extent that continuation of the trial is no longer feasible can be ordered removed by the court. An example of this occurred in the case of Bobby Seale in the dramatic so-called Chicago Seven Conspiracy trial in the U.S. where during a part of the case Seale was bound and gagged by court officers when the judge decided he was unduly interrupting the proceedings.

When there is a trial of the issue of whether the accused is unfit to stand trial by reason of insanity, the trial judge can order the accused kept out of court if satisfied that the accused's presence in court may have an adverse affect on his or her mental health.

Recent amendments to the Criminal Code also provide for the continuation of a trial or preliminary hearing in the absence of an accused who has absconded during the course of the proceeding. In such cases the Code deems that the accused has waived his or her right to be present, and the court may continue the trial and proceed to the point of committal for trial in the case of a preliminary hearing or proceed to judgment or verdict in the case of trial and impose a sentence in the absence of the accused.

The alternative that is always available to the court is to issue a warrant and await the arrest of the accused. In all such cases, counsel for the accused is entitled to continue to act for the absent accused in the proceedings.

c. THE TRIAL OF CORPORATIONS

Corporations are legal persons under Canadian law and can be liable for the acts of their directors and other persons managing their business when such acts are criminal and occur within the business affairs of the company. Service of a summons, notice, or other process on a corporation can be effected by delivering the process to the manager, secretary, or other executive officer of the corporation or of a branch.

A corporation must appear by its counsel or an agent on an indictable offence. Where the corporation does not appear by counsel or agent, and service of the summons upon the corporation is proved, the judge may, if the offence is one over which he or she has absolute jurisdiction, proceed with the trial in the absence of the corporation or hold a preliminary hearing if it is an electable offence.

Where a corporation is ordered to stand trial following a preliminary hearing, and an indictment has been preferred, the clerk of the court must serve a copy of the indictment upon the corporation. A notice must accompany the indictment, stating the nature and claims of the indictment and advising that, unless the corporation appears and pleads within seven days after service of the notice, a plea of not guilty will be entered and the trial will proceed as though the corporation had appeared and pleaded.

If the corporation does not appear, the presiding judge may, after proof of service of the notice, order the court clerk to enter a plea of not guilty.

There is, of course, no provision for imprisoning a corporation. The difficulty of a corporation having no actual physical being was a considerable problem at common law when at one time all felonies were punishable by death. As the corporation was incapable of suffering the prescribed punishment, there was no point in putting it on trial.

However, our contemporary Criminal Code deals with this by providing that a convicted corporation shall be fined in an amount that is in the discretion of the court in any indictable offence, and an amount not exceeding $25 000 for a summary offence.

These fines can be enforced by the prosecutor filing the conviction in the superior court and entering as a judgment the amount of the fine and costs, if any, which are ordered. Such judgment is enforceable against the corporation in the same manner as if it were obtained in civil proceedings.

d. TRIAL IN OPEN COURT

The general rule is that criminal trials must be held in open court and there must be some sign or markings identifying the court as a courtroom. Failure to hold a trial in open court may provide an accused person with valid grounds of appeal.

However, there are certain restrictive circumstances in which the trial can be held *in camera*. This will be the case where the judge is of the view that it is in the interest of public morals, maintenance of order, or proper administration of justice to exclude the public.

In the case of a sexual offence against a female where the judge has granted the accused's lawyer the right to question the complainant about her previous sexual conduct, the presiding judge must give reasons for this decision if he or she does not exclude the public.

There is specific provision that the trial of an accused person under the age of 16 years must take place without publicity. This is a rare situation because such cases are normally governed by the Young Offenders Act, except where the youth has been transferred to adult court (see chapter 32).

e. THE PRESUMPTION OF INNOCENCE

Any person charged with a criminal offence has the right to "be presumed innocent until proven guilty according to law in a fair and public hearing by an independent and impartial tribunal." This constitutional right is guaranteed by Section 11(d) of the Charter of Rights and Freedoms.

Innocence is presumed at the time the accused is charged and continues to be presumed until the Crown has proved the criminal offence beyond a reasonable doubt. If the judge or jury, as the case may be, has a reasonable doubt, that doubt must be exercised in favor of the accused because of the presumption of innocence.

f. RIGHT TO REMAIN SILENT

In Canada, an accused person is entitled to remain silent at his or her trial. No accused person can be required by the Crown to give evidence. This right is enshrined in Section 11(c) of the Charter of Rights and Freedoms.

The Crown must prove its case against the accused. The accused is not required to do anything. He or she can remain silent throughout the trial and at the end argue that the Crown has not proved its case beyond a reasonable doubt.

g. THE RIGHT TO MAKE FULL ANSWER AND DEFENCE

If you are the accused, you have the right to make full answer and defence to the case advanced by the Crown. This includes the right to cross examine and contradict the Crown witnesses. The judge must hear evidence on behalf of the defence if it is relevant to the charge and must hear defence submissions and motions to dismiss the charge.

h. COURTROOM MANNERS

The judge is supreme in the courtroom and has a wide discretion to regulate the proceedings and to rule on evidence, adjournments, arguments, and so forth.

As noted above, judicial proceedings in Canada are quite formal and it is a good practice to conduct yourself appropriately by dressing neatly and by behaving calmly.

Such acts as verbal outbursts, eating, chewing gum, drinking coffee, or smoking a cigarette in a courtroom may lead the judge to consider an immediate citation for contempt in the face of the court. The judge may feel that these matters violate the decorum of the courtroom and a usual and predictable reaction will be to tell you to leave the courtroom, although the judge does have power to immediately request that you show cause why you should not be cited for contempt. You should avoid doing anything that the court may consider contemptuous.

Lawyers or other people making arguments to judges or juries are entitled to put their best foot forward, to argue strongly and convincingly, and to stand their ground. Indeed, the courtroom is seldom a place for timidity as it is essential to present your case as strongly as possible. However, this must also be done with the judge and jury in mind, and appropriate respect should be shown for them, for court staff, and for Crown lawyers.

Judges are not permitted by law to indicate any bias against a particular defendant. A judge's comments must relate only to the proceedings and the evidence before him or her and to the legal issues that arise.

The judge is not entitled to comment on the color of a person's skin or say anything that indicates prejudice. If the judge does show any bias, the defendant's lawyer may be able to take steps in the higher courts to have the conviction, if any, quashed, or to stop the proceedings in order to get a new judge or a new trial.

i. MISTRIALS AND HUNG JURIES

A mistrial may occur if some gravely prejudicial and inadmissible evidence has reached the jury and the judge thinks it may have contaminated the jury against the defendant.

The practical effect of a mistrial is that the judge will discharge the present jury and adjourn the case for the purpose of getting a new jury to hear it. It may be adjourned to the next session of court, which may be several months away.

A hung jury arises where the judge is satisfied that the jury is unable to agree upon a verdict (they must be unanimous), and that keeping them further would be useless. In such a case, the judge may again discharge the jury and direct a new jury to be empanelled during the sittings of the court and adjourn the case on such terms as justice may require.

j. APPEALS

The subject of appeals is beyond the scope of this book. It is sufficient to say that a convicted person is entitled to appeal from conviction in both summary and indictable proceedings. In indictable proceedings the appeal goes directly to the provincial court of appeal. In summary proceedings the appeal will be to the county or district court or, in certain circumstances, to the superior court; there may be a further appeal to the court of appeal.

There is generally a right of appeal to the Supreme Court of Canada in Ottawa on all cases where questions of law are involved and the court grants leave, or where one of the judges of the court of appeal has dissented from the others on a question of law, in which case there is an appeal as of right.

There are also appeals from sentence up to the provincial court of appeal level. There are no sentence appeals in the Supreme Court of Canada.

28
THE RIGHTS OF WITNESSES

So far we have been concerned only with the civil rights of suspects and accused persons. A far greater number of people will have contact with the criminal law process as sources of information or witnesses.

Sometimes a witness may be a suspect, depending on his or her relationship to the accused and connection with the suspected crime. In such cases, it is particularly important for you to know your civil rights for self-protection.

In addition, there are many cases where a witness, although not under suspicion for the crime alleged against the accused, may be concerned about divulging information on his or her past activities to police or prosecutors. That is, there may be matters which would form part of your testimony as a witness and which might expose you to embarrassment, prejudice, loss of a job, or some form of civil or criminal legal liability.

a. THE RIGHT OF A WITNESS TO HAVE A LAWYER

A witness is not protected from testifying merely because such testimony may be incriminating. However, if you are contacted by police as a potential witness during an investigation, you are entitled to consult with a lawyer before speaking to the police.

There are no protections that police can guarantee to a witness who gives incriminating information. Police do not grant any right against self-incrimination when they interview a witness; this right can only be asserted in court. The only right you have at an initial interview with the police is the right to remain silent and not to incriminate yourself. No witness can be compelled to answer incriminating questions out of court. Hence, the first priority in such circumstances may be to consult with a lawyer.

The lawyer will be able to advise whether there is any potential risk to you in answering police questions. It may be possible to arrange a meeting involving you, your lawyer, and the police officer. In this context the lawyer can intervene to halt questioning, to advise you, or to answer on your behalf if there is a danger of self-incrimination.

The lawyer will find out from the police the purpose of the interview and perhaps extract a guarantee that you will not be prosecuted, or the lawyer may caution you not to answer any questions at this time.

b. WITNESS UNDER SUBPOENA

A subpoena is a court document requiring you to appear at a trial to give evidence. It can only be issued properly where you are "likely to give material evidence" in a criminal proceeding. It must be under the seal of the court issuing it and must be signed by a judge of the court or a clerk of the court.

A subpoena must state the name of the case and the charge against the named accused. It will contain a command to appear before a judge of a certain court at a date and time specified to give evidence.

c. SUBPOENA OF DOCUMENTS

A subpoena may specify that you are to produce any documents in your possession or under your control which relate to the charge. It may specify the particular documents or it may leave it to you to decide whether the documents relate to the charge.

The subpoena must be served personally upon the person to whom it is directed, although it may be left at his or her place of residence with some person who appears to be at least 16 years old.

d. MATERIAL WITNESS WARRANT

Where it appears to the prosecutor that a person likely to give material evidence will not attend court in response to a subpoena, or is evading service of a subpoena, the prosecutor may apply to the judge for a warrant for the arrest of the potential witness. This is commonly referred to as a material witness warrant.

A warrant would also be used if a witness, who was served with a subpoena or arrested as a material witness and released on a recognizance, failed to appear or remain at the trial until excused, or if he or she absconded or planned to abscond.

If you are in this situation, the general procedure is that when you are arrested you must be brought before the judge immediately. The judge will then determine whether to release you on a recognizance to appear when required, or keep you in custody until you have testified.

However, no person can be held more than 30 days on a material witness warrant without a judge reviewing the matter further. Additionally, you or your lawyer can initiate a review of your detention at any time before the expiry of 30 days.

The total period for which a witness can be held must not exceed 90 days. Failing to attend court as required or to remain in court may amount to a contempt of court, bringing a fine of up to $100 or up to 90 days imprisonment, and possibly payment of costs of the proceedings.

e. ATTACKING THE SUBPOENA

A subpoena may be attacked in superior court by a motion to quash. If the subpoena appears to be invalid in its form, it may be attacked on this ground.

It also may be attacked on the basis that the witness is not likely to give material evidence and that Crown counsel is on a fishing expedition and does not legitimately require the witness's evidence for the particular case or for any other legal reason.

f. REFUSAL OF WITNESS TO ANSWER QUESTIONS

A witness who appears at a preliminary hearing or trial and refuses to answer questions may be jailed for up to eight days. The judge must resume the trial before expiry of the eight-day period, but if you still refuse to answer, the judge may commit you to custody for a further period not exceeding eight days.

In theory, the judge can continue to do this, although in practice Crown counsel or defence counsel, whichever side is not relying on the witness' testimony, would probably urge the judge against granting a further adjournment.

Alternatively, a trial judge may summarily find a refusal to answer questions to be a contempt in the face of the court and impose punishment of a fine or period of imprisonment. This is an alternative to the eight-day custody remands; the law does not permit the same witness to be subject to double jeopardy.

g. TAKING THE OATH

A witness is not required to swear on the Bible to tell the truth. You are entitled to object on the basis of conscientious scruples to the taking of an oath. If you do not wish to be sworn, you should simply advise the judge that you would like to affirm. The judge will receive the evidence as being under oath where a witness solemnly affirms to tell the truth.

A child may give evidence. A child who understands the oath may be sworn or affirmed. A child of "tender years" who does not understand the oath may be sworn if he or she appears to be reasonably intelligent and understands the duty of telling the truth. However, the law provides that no person can be convicted on the unsworn evidence of a child unless it is materially corroborated by other evidence.

h. HUSBAND OR WIFE AS WITNESS

In most criminal cases, the Crown is not entitled to compel the husband to be a witness against the wife, or the wife to be a witness against the husband. There is a common law exception to this rule where the crime involves violence or a threat of violence to the other spouse, or where the crime involves youths, such as contributing to youth delinquency, molesting children, and so on.

Other exceptions to the rule that a spouse cannot be compelled to testify against the other spouse are in cases of —

- rape,
- attempted rape,
- sexual intercourse with a female under 16 years of age,
- sexual intercourse with a feeble-minded person,
- incest,
- seduction of a female between 16 and 18,
- seduction under promise of marriage,
- sexual intercourse with a step-daughter or female employee,
- seduction of female passengers on vessels,
- buggery or bestiality,
- gross indecency,
- parent or guardian procuring defilement of a child under their care,
- householder permitting defilement of a female child under their care,
- corrupting children,
- indecent acts,
- vagrancy,
- procuring,
- failing to provide necessaries to a person under one's charge,
- abandoning a child,
- abduction of a female,

- abduction of a child under 14,
- procuring a feigned marriage,
- pretending to solemnize marriage,
- bigamy or polygamy,
- theft between husband and wife,
- conspiracy to commit murder.

However, even in those cases where it is possible to compel one spouse as a witness against the other spouse, no spouse is compelled to disclose any statement or communication made by the other spouse during the course of the marriage. This means that no husband can be compelled to disclose anything said by his wife during the marriage, and no wife can be compelled to disclose anything said to her by her husband during the marriage.

i. THE ACCUSED AS WITNESS

An accused person has an absolute right not to testify. Many innocent people with a bad demeanor are their own worst enemy at their trial. There are many cases in which it is better not to testify.

In some cases, the Crown may have a weak or circumstantial case and your testimony may fill in missing pieces of evidence in the Crown's case. In other cases, your manner or demeanor as a witness may cause the judge or jury to disbelieve your evidence and ultimately the testimony may harm the case more than help it.

Under Canadian law an accused person is entitled to remain entirely mute and communicate at the trial only through counsel, except for pleading not guilty to the charge.

j. SOLICITOR/CLIENT PRIVILEGE

Communication between a solicitor and his or her client is absolutely privileged in the sense that the client has an absolute right to privacy. The lawyer has no right to waive the secrecy of such communication, although the client may do so if he or she wishes.

There is an exception where such communication is intended to help commit a crime; no person can use a lawyer as an instrument to commit a crime. Apart from this exception, there is no need to disclose any communication to a lawyer, and the lawyer is not entitled to divulge any communication made by a client unless the client waives that privilege.

k. SELF-INCRIMINATION

Section 13 of the Charter of Rights and Freedoms provides that a witness who testifies in any proceedings has the right "not to have any incriminating evidence so given used to incriminate that witness in any other proceedings, except in a prosecution for perjury or for the giving of contradictory evidence." This is a new constitutional protection against future use of self-incriminating statements made by a witness.

It is not clear how far this constitutional protection extends. For example, does it cover an accused person who, in the course of testifying at his or her trial, reveals evidence of different crimes than the one being charged? Is it restricted to evidence that is directly incriminating, as opposed to evidence that, when put together with other incriminating evidence, may be incriminating? These questions will probably not be resolved for a few years.

It is important to note that the protection in Section 5 of the Canada Evidence Act has been left intact. That is, a witness who is asked a potentially incriminating question can object on the grounds that the answer may tend to incriminate. The judge can then order the question to be answered, although the answer cannot be used in any subsequent proceeding.

This protection is not nearly as broad as the protection under the fifth amendment in the United States Constitution. Under the U.S. system, the Canadian rule is referred to as "use immunity." That is, a particular answer may not be used against the witness in any subsequent civil or criminal proceeding.

However, the Americans also have what is called "transactional immunity," which is not available under Canadian law. It provides that the crime on which the witness is being questioned cannot be charged against the accused at a future date.

In Canada, anything learned about a witness when he or she is in the witness box can be used against the witness for the purpose of investigation and criminal charges, although a specific answer cannot be used as evidence against the witness.

1. OBSTRUCTION OF JUSTICE

Any person who wilfully attempts to obstruct, pervert, or defeat the course of justice by using threats, bribes, or other corrupt means to dissuade or attempt to dissuade a person from being a witness may be charged with an indictable offence carrying a maximum penalty of 10 years in jail.

29
ROLE OF THE PRESS IN CRIMINAL PROCEEDINGS: PUBLICATION AND BROADCAST OF EVIDENCE OF PROCEEDINGS

Section 2 of the Charter of Rights and Freedoms provides that everyone has the fundamental freedoms of "thought, belief, opinion and expression, including freedom of the press and other media of communication."

A balancing act is performed by the courts in, on the one hand, safeguarding our right of free expression, and on the other hand, safeguarding an accused person's right to a fair trial.

Freedom of the press includes the right to investigate, report, and editorialize; and these rights extend to reports of judicial proceedings.

However, there are some obvious limits on the exercise of these rights, such as the defamatory libel laws and contempt laws.

In addition, in a criminal case, once proceedings have been started against an accused person, the press must be extremely careful in deciding what to print or broadcast. At this stage, society demands that a fair trial for the accused be given some priority. Accordingly, an accused or his or her counsel may exercise certain rights to restrict pre-trial or *sub judice* publication.

The following are examples of statutory limitations on press freedom in the course of criminal proceedings.

a. LIMITS ON THE PRESS AFTER ARREST OF THE ACCUSED: CRIMINAL CONTEMPT

At common law, any action which would have the effect of prejudicing the fair trial of a pending proceeding, whether civil or criminal, is a contempt. Many cases are the result of comment in newspapers and magazines or on television or radio on pending cases and the parties to them.

Criminal proceedings are pending from the law's point of view from the moment you are arrested and are in custody, though you have not yet been brought before any court. In fact, there have been cases in which it was contempt to publish information about a person who was at the time suspected, though not yet arrested or charged with an offence.

The proceedings continue to be pending until the appeals have been exhausted, although the problem is more serious when proceedings are pending before a jury than before appeal judges.

Contempt arises if the publication creates a real possibility of prejudice to the fair hearing of the matter. In previous cases, some of the following principles have been established:

(a) Any statement suggesting that an accused person is guilty of the offence charged, or has confessed to it, or has been guilty of other offences may amount to contempt.

(b) It is contempt for a newspaper to conduct and publish the results of an independent investigation into a crime for which a person has been arrested.

(c) Publication of a photograph of an accused where it is reasonably clear that the question of his or her identity with the criminal has arisen or may arise may be contempt.

In such cases, the contempt is a contempt out of court. Proceedings are normally initiated by Crown counsel issuing writs of attachment against the reporter and his or her newspaper or radio or television station for contempt of court on stated grounds.

The usual grounds will include that in publicly making those statements in reference to the accused person, the defendants acted in a manner calculated to interfere with the due administration of justice. Where the court finds the contempt, it may impose fines on the corporation involved and a fine or imprisonment upon the individual reporter.

b. WHAT IS THE PRESS ENTITLED TO PUBLISH?

The press is always entitled to publish the fact that you have been charged and the specific nature of the charges against you. They can state such matters as the date and place of arrest, your occupation, the date set for court appearance or bail hearing, and the names of the defence lawyer and the prosecutor.

Care is required in describing the crime so as not to make any suggestion that the person charged may have committed the crime.

c. REPORTING OF BAIL HEARING

In any bail hearing where the prosecutor is attempting to argue that you should be released on some basis other than a simple undertaking or should be detained in custody, or where you are arguing that you should not be detained in custody, you are entitled to apply for an order directing that the evidence and submissions and the reasons given by the judge not be published in any newspaper or broadcast until a preliminary hearing is held and you are discharged or the trial is ended.

The term "newspaper" is defined as including any paper, magazine, or periodical containing public news, intelligence, or reports of events. Disobeying the order for non-broadcast or non-publication is a summary offence punishable by a fine of up to $2 000, or up to six months in jail, or both.

The section leaves it open to the press to publish the name of the person applying for bail, the names of the lawyers involved, the details of the charge, the amount of bail granted, whether sureties are involved or not, or whether there was a detention order made and the date to which the case has been remanded.

It is directed at preventing the publication of any information called by the prosecutor tending to show that the accused might be guilty of the crime. This type of information could contaminate a possible juror and could turn public opinion against the accused person.

d. AT THE PRELIMINARY HEARING

The press is entitled to publish the fact of any remands or adjournments up to the time of the preliminary hearing. If any applications are made in open court, such as an application to adjourn the trial or preliminary hearing, the circumstances of such application can be published unless the judge orders otherwise.

However, at the beginning of the preliminary hearing, counsel for the accused is entitled to request an order directing that the evidence taken at the hearing not be published in any newspaper or broadcast on radio or television before the discharge of the accused or until the trial is ended.

A violation of this order will again lead to a summary conviction offence, potentially involving a charge against both the corporation and the individual.

The question again arises, what is the press entitled to publish at this stage? The public is clearly interested and has a right to know whether you have been committed to stand trial or discharged at the preliminary hearing. In fact, the press is entitled to publish this information.

The order that can be obtained in this case is only directed at the evidence taken at the inquiry. There is nothing to prevent the press from publishing the fact that the judge discharged or committed you for trial and his or her statements in so doing.

Of course, if you are discharged at the preliminary hearing, the press could also publish the evidence of the hearing. If you are committed for trial, the press can publish that fact, along with the description of the charges, the length of the hearing, the number of witnesses called, names of counsel, potential trial dates, and the date of next appearance.

e. PUBLICATION OR BROADCAST OF A CONFESSION

Even where defence lawyers do not apply for an order of non-publication or non-broadcast of the evidence at the preliminary hearing, there is another section of the Criminal Code which forbids a newspaper or television or radio station from publishing or broadcasting any report of a confession or admission given in evidence at a preliminary hearing until your discharge or the end of the trial. This is a separate offence and will result in summary conviction charges against the offenders.

This is based on the premise that even the report of a confession given in evidence might prejudice the case against you. There are good reasons for this: at the trial you may take the position that such admission or confession was illegally obtained by police and should not be part of the evidence.

The rules on illegally obtained confessions are based on the view that such confessions, having been obtained through threats or inducements, might be false and should not be considered by the jury.

During the trial, the issue of whether a confession was obtained by police through legal methods or illegal methods is determined in the absence of the jury. It is a criminal contempt for any newspaper or radio or television station to broadcast a report of evidence or proceedings which occur in the absence of the jury.

If a confession is ruled to be legally obtained and relevant to the case, the evidence will be led again in front of the jury. Otherwise, the law requires that such material not reach the jury.

f. MOTION FOR CHANGE OF VENUE

You have the right to be tried in the county or district in which the offence alleged against you was committed. However, every superior court or court of criminal jurisdiction may try you where you are arrested or are in custody, provided that is within the territorial jurisdiction of the court.

The place of the trial is known at common law as the "venue of the trial." Under Section 527 of the Criminal Code, the prosecutor or the accused has the right to apply for a change of venue in the court where indicted or before a judge who may sit in that court.

The judge may order the trial to be held in another territory of the province if it appears expedient to the ends of justice, although you must establish more than a mere possibility of prejudice. Where you can establish reasonable probability of prejudice, perhaps as a result of adverse comment in a local newspaper, a change of venue may be granted.

Premature publication of a statement or confession in the local press before the trial may be a ground for a change of venue.

In one case, a change of venue was granted after a former application for a change of venue, which had been dismissed, was publicized widely in a newspaper having huge circulation in the county. The court was concerned that the accused might not have a fair trial as a result of a prospective jury being informed that the accused mistrusted their fairness and that of other citizens of the county and made an application to change the venue.

g. MOTION FOR MISTRIAL

Once the arraignment is complete and the trial has begun, wide dissemination of prejudicial comment may lead counsel for the accused to make a motion for a mistrial.

A judge who is satisfied that there is a definite danger that the jury has been contaminated by the prejudicial reports, may declare a mistrial. He or she might then adjourn the case, and the defence may apply for a change of venue.

h. PUBLICATION OF EVIDENCE DURING TRIAL

The media are entitled to report the proceedings and evidence during the course of a trial, provided such proceedings or evidence do not occur in the absence of the jury.

Such reports of proceedings and evidence are frequently very detailed and the law permits even the publication of verbatim statements of the evidence. In fact, the Criminal Code contains a positive protection for the press against charges of defamatory libel provided that the publisher can show that the matter was published in good faith, for the information of the public, and was a part of public proceedings before a court exercising judicial authority or fair comment upon any such proceedings.

30
DISCHARGES, CONVICTIONS, AND SENTENCES

In many cases, a judge may find an accused person guilty but decline to enter a conviction against that person. This arises from the trial judge's powers to grant a conditional or absolute discharge to a person who has pleaded guilty or been found guilty.

Wherever the offence is one punishable by a maximum penalty of less than 14 years in jail, the court may discharge you absolutely or conditionally instead of convicting you. Eligible offences include: all charges of theft or possession of stolen property, all charges of obtaining by false pretences, fraud charges, all Food and Drugs Act offences, all charges of simple possession of narcotics (whether for heroin, cocaine, or cannabis), all summary offences (such as causing a disturbance, unlawful assembly, soliciting, common assault), charges of assault causing bodily harm, and assaulting, obstructing, or resisting a police officer.

a. ABSOLUTE AND CONDITIONAL DISCHARGES

The effect of an absolute discharge is that the accused, although found guilty of the offence, walks out of the courtroom with no conviction and no penalty.

The court can also impose a conditional discharge wherein there will be a probation order, and the accused will be directed to comply with the conditions of the probation order. The effect of this discharge is that you are deemed not to have been convicted of the offence to which you pleaded or were found guilty.

The conditional and absolute discharges are curious additions to our criminal law. Can a person who gets a conditional discharge honestly say he or she has no criminal record? Or can that person only say that he or she has no convictions?

The traditional approach is that you do not have a criminal record unless convicted of a criminal offence. Therefore, it would seem logical that people who have been discharged have not been convicted and, therefore, have no criminal record. This would be the best approach for a discharged person to take.

Potential employers with whom a discharged person may come into contact may not fully appreciate the impact of a technicality that Parliament has passed into law. It is better to tell them you have no criminal record, if you must comment on it at all.

It is clear that the absolute and conditional discharges have been invoked to stem or control the rising tide of "criminals" resulting from great numbers of minor violations of the drug laws.

The use of marijuana, hashish, cocaine, and other drugs is now so widespread that many people who might otherwise have no contact with the criminal justice system have appeared before the courts on these charges. With the discharge provisions, these types of offences will not necessarily result in a conviction. The courts can avoid convicting violators if they feel that a particular person should not have a criminal record.

b. WHAT WILL THE JUDGE CONSIDER ON AN APPLICATION FOR DISCHARGE?

When an accused person or his or her lawyer applies to a judge for a conditional or absolute discharge, the judge must decide whether it is in the best interests of the accused person and not contrary to the public interest. There are few cases where a discharge would not be in the best interests of the accused. However, the judge will consider some or all of the following matters:

(a) Age of the accused (Generally the courts are prone to give a younger person a second chance.)

(b) Circumstances of the alleged offence (Are there factors that show he or she might deserve a discharge?)

(c) Potential adverse consequences to employment or a possible professional career (Is there evidence that this particular accused may suffer more than others from a conviction?)

(d) Evidence of genuine remorse or rehabilitation (Is the accused a person who will not get into trouble again?)

(e) Evidence of good character

(f) Opinion of a probation officer in a pre-sentence report (Not always requested by the judge, but will usually have a strong effect on the judge's thinking.)

(g) Any other matters that might be relevant in a given case (Some judges will consider a person's immigration status, if conviction for the particular offence may create problems for him or her and if the person is otherwise leading a productive life.)

A judge will also consider whether the discharge would be contrary to the public interest. If there is anything about the offence or the offender that indicates a flagrant disregard for the law, this will certainly be a basis for a judge to refuse a discharge.

At times, a particular offence may be on the increase in a particular locality; this will have an influence on the judge. A number of other factors, such as whether an offence was carried out with planning and deliberation or whether it had an element of viciousness to it will also influence a judge.

c. WHEN YOU ARE CONVICTED

Once you have been convicted of an offence, you will be sentenced by the judge. If you are youthful or if it is your first offence, there will probably be a probation report.

If the crime of which you were convicted is not aggravated, you will likely be given a discharge, if eligible, or a suspended sentence and placed on probation for a period up to three years. In appropriate cases, fines or short terms of jail will be imposed.

For some offences a jail term is mandatory and for many other offences a jail term is very likely. However, each case is different. There can be considerable variation in sentence from one case to another even though the charge is the same.

d. INTERMITTENT SENTENCES

The Criminal Code has provision for intermittent jail sentences where the total amount of imprisonment does not exceed 90 days. This means that a person who is working or going to school may continue to do so during the week and serve the jail term on weekends.

Formerly, people who were sent to jail were forced into isolation and were cut off completely from the community. This meant loss of friends, relationships, employment, and activities. Now, accused persons who are fortunate enough to receive intermittent sentences can continue to support their family or pursue their career or education while serving a short jail term.

e. THE ABOLITION OF CAPITAL PUNISHMENT

On July 16, 1976, the bill abolishing capital punishment became effective. It created the new crimes of first degree and second degree murder and the offence of high treason.

While abolishing capital punishment, it created a mandatory 25-year jail term (without parole) for convictions of first degree murder. This includes killing prison guards, police officials, contract killings, and killings in the commission of offences such as hijacking or rape.

It also provided that a person convicted of other murder, now second degree murder, could be required to serve up to 25 years in jail without parole.

31
CRIMINAL RECORDS

Any conviction under the Criminal Code or other federal statute will leave you with a criminal record. No distinction is made between a summary or an indictable offence. The record is tied to you by your name, a number, and your fingerprints and photographs, if they have been taken.

a. CONSEQUENCES OF A CRIMINAL RECORD

There are a number of adverse effects from a criminal record. One or more of the following consequences could arise:

(a) Loss of employment opportunity. For example, a conviction for theft or fraud may prevent you from obtaining employment in a position of trust or any position where it may be necessary to be bonded by insurers. In addition, there is the possibility that any employer who learns of the criminal conviction may refuse to hire or may fire you. Relief may be available under provincial and federal human rights legislation.

The key issue will be whether the conviction relates to the employment, occupation, or membership in question. If it does not, you may have a legal remedy against the employer, professional body, or trade union.

(b) Loss of economic opportunity. For example, a business licence for certain endeavors or a liquor licence may be withheld in the case of convictions reflecting on character and reputation. Legal remedies are available for a person who is the victim of unreasonable discrimination.

(c) Loss of the right to vote or to be a candidate for public office in the case of a person who is incarcerated for a criminal conviction, or people who have been convicted of illegal or corrupt electoral practices.

(d) In court, a criminal record will affect bail and sentencing in any subsequent case. A record makes it more likely that a prosecutor will seek a high bail or a detention order for an accused person. It will also affect the thinking of a trial judge at the time sentence is passed for a subsequent offence. Here again, one consideration will be whether there is any similarity between the present offence and the previous conviction.

(e) If you are a Canadian citizen, a criminal record will not affect your right to a Canadian passport, although it may affect your right to enter a foreign country. If you are a citizen of another country applying to enter Canada, a criminal record may prevent you from gaining landed immigrant status. If you are a permanent resident, a conviction may hinder an application for citizenship.

b. APPLICATION FOR PARDON

Under the Criminal Records Act, any person who has been convicted of a summary offence is entitled to apply for a pardon two years after completion of the sentence; that is, after a period of probation or term of imprisonment has expired, or a fine has been paid, whichever happens last.

People convicted of indictable offences can also apply for a pardon, but must wait until five years after completion of the sentence.

The Criminal Records Act also applies to a person who has been granted an absolute or conditional discharge. Where an absolute discharge is granted for a summary offence, the application for pardon may be made one year after the date on which the discharge was given.

In the case of a conditional discharge, an application for a pardon can be made one year from the date of termination of the period of probation. In the case of indictable offences, the application can be made three years after that date of an absolute discharge or three years after the completion of a period of probation in a conditional discharge.

An application for pardon is made to the Solicitor General of Canada. It is a fairly brief form, requiring particulars of family status and details of employment since the conviction.

You must give a brief description of the circumstances of each criminal conviction and provide at least five people to whom a National Parole Service investigator may refer in confidence.

The department cautions applicants to advise them if a relative, employer, or employee is not aware of the conviction. The applicant must agree that the information provided may be forwarded on a confidential basis to law enforcement agencies.

The National Parole Board normally takes several months to process an application, checking the background of the applicant, interviewing past and present employers, law officers, and other persons given as references.

Where the Parole Board does not agree that a pardon should be granted, it must notify the applicant and advise that he or she is entitled to make oral or written representations to the Board. The ultimate power to grant a pardon lies with the Cabinet, acting on the advice of the Parole Board.

c. EFFECT OF A PARDON

The pardon simply stands as proof that the National Parole Board, after making proper inquiries, is satisfied that the applicant is of good behavior and that the conviction should no longer reflect adversely on his or her character.

It removes any remaining disqualification from the point of view of federal statutes or regulations. It does not necessarily have any effect on provincial laws, or on the rules that an employer (except the federal government) might apply, provided they are legal under provincial law.

A pardon can be revoked if the person is convicted of a further offence or on the basis of evidence that the person is no longer of good conduct or that the pardon was obtained by false or deceptive statements.

d. IS THERE A CRIMINAL RECORD WHERE A PERSON IS ACQUITTED?

There is no criminal record in the usual sense for a person who was charged and then acquitted, or if a stay of proceedings was entered or a charge was withdrawn. Technically, the charge doesn't give you any kind of criminal record unless it results in a conviction.

For court purposes, a charge which results in an acquittal cannot be raised again; however, data showing the date and place of the charge or arrest and the disposition remains in the permanent records of the Royal Canadian Mounted Police.

The RCMP identification branch in Ottawa will tell you that only convictions are on your record and that if you don't have a conviction, you don't have a record. This is not strictly true.

For example, a person who has been arrested for possession of marijuana, fingerprinted and photographed, put on trial and acquitted, will have a permanent file with the RCMP in Ottawa, despite the fact of the acquittal.

Under present administrative procedures, it is quite conceivable that that information would be available to any police officer in the RCMP or the police force of any major city who is making a routine check of that individual at a later date. It is information that may influence a police officer to search a driver's vehicle in a case where it would not otherwise be done. In this sense it can lead to a search without proper grounds.

In addition, the fact that a person has been charged and acquitted is available to prosecutors and may be used as a guideline in deciding whether or not to lay a charge in a marginal case.

e. REQUEST TO DESTROY FINGERPRINTS AND PHOTOGRAPHS

A person who has been fingerprinted and photographed is entitled to apply to the RCMP to have the fingerprints or photographs destroyed following an acquittal on the charge.

Where an independent police agency took the photographs and fingerprints, the RCMP prefer that the application for destruction be made initially to that other police force, which will then transmit it to the RCMP.

This remedy is available as well in any case on which the Crown had the option of proceeding by way of summary or indictable charge, and opted to proceed by summary proceedings. This would apply in the vast majority of cases of possession of a narcotic, or drug under the Food and Drugs Act, as well as on charges of impaired driving and related offences.

32
YOUNG OFFENDERS

The Young Offenders Act applies to persons under 18 years of age who are charged with criminal offences. A "young person" is defined as a person who appears to be over 12 years of age, but under 18 years of age. A person under the age of 12 years is defined as a "child," and cannot be charged with a criminal offence even in youth court.

a. WHAT OFFENCES ARE DEALT WITH IN YOUTH COURT?

It is important to remember that the Young Offenders Act applies only to young people charged with criminal offences under *federal* legislation. Each province has other laws respecting young people. For example, each province may set a different age under provincial laws at which a minor can drive a motor vehicle, smoke cigarettes, see restricted movies, or drink alcohol.

If you want information about any of these provincial laws, you could write to the attorney general or justice minister of the province or consult legal aid services.

A person under 18 years of age could be charged in adult court with a provincial offence of being a minor in possession of liquor, even though he or she could not be charged in adult court with any federal criminal offence.

The former offence of delinquency, under the now-repealed Juvenile Delinquents Act, included violations of provincial statutes or city by-laws, but the new act is restricted to matters generally considered to be criminal.

b. POLICY OF THE LAW IN DEALING WITH YOUNG OFFENDERS

The Young Offenders Act contains a declaration of principle that sets out its objectives. These objectives include that young people must be responsible for their contraventions of law, though not to the same degree as adults; that young persons require discipline and control, but also guidance and assistance; that in some cases it is appropriate to take measures other than criminal charges; that young people have all the rights and freedoms contained in the Charter of Rights and Freedoms and have the right to be informed of their rights; that the rights of young persons include a right to the least possible interference with freedom that is consistent with the protection of society; and that young offenders should only be removed from their parents' care when absolutely necessary.

c. ARREST OF YOUNG OFFENDERS

The laws of arrest, search and seizure for young offenders are basically the same as those for adult offenders.

All the provisions of the Criminal Code apply, with appropriate modifications, to offences alleged to have been committed by young persons. This means the laws of arrest that are discussed in chapter 3 apply to young offenders.

A young offender who is arrested and detained should inform the police or youth court authorities of his or her legal age as soon as possible. A youth court judge can release an arrested young person to a responsible adult who is willing and able to care for and supervise the young person.

It is important that the young offender who is taken to a detention centre provide the name, telephone number, and address of his or her parents. This will help in obtaining release.

Often young offender cases do not proceed to arrest or court appearance, but where they do, there will normally be an order releasing the young person to the care of the parent. The court has power to set bail in the same way that an adult court does, but usually avoids doing so unless the circumstances are aggravated, or there is a possibility that the young person may skip bail, or commit further offences.

If the arrested young person is a runaway, or the parents claim the child is unmanageable, the court will try to find a suitable group home or foster parents. Detention pending trial will be viewed as a last resort.

d. FINGERPRINTING AND PHOTOGRAPHING OF YOUNG OFFENDERS

Section 44 of the Young Offenders Act gives police the power to fingerprint and photograph young persons charged with an indictable offence. However, the act stipulates that no photographs or fingerprints shall be taken of a young person who is accused of committing an offence except in the circumstances in which an adult may, under the Identification of Criminals Act, be subjected to the measures, processes, and operations referred to in that Act.

e. RIGHT TO COUNSEL

A young person has the right to retain and instruct counsel without delay at any stage of the court proceeding.

The arresting officer must advise the young person of the right to be represented by counsel, and must provide an opportunity for the youth to obtain counsel. In addition, where a young person is not represented by a lawyer at youth court proceedings, the judge must advise the young person of the right to counsel and provide a reasonable opportunity to obtain counsel. If the young person requires legal aid, the court must refer him or her to the legal aid program or direct that counsel be appointed, in which case the attorney general must arrange for counsel to represent the young person.

In cases where the youth court judge perceives that the interests of the alleged young offender and his or her parents are in conflict, the judge must ensure that separate legal representation, independent of the parents, is given to the young person.

f. NOTICE TO PARENTS

The young person's parents must be given notice of his or her arrest, place of detention and the reason for the arrest. In addition, the parents must be given notice of any documents requiring the youth to appear in court.

If the whereabouts of the parents is not known, or if the parents are unavailable, the notice may be given to an adult relative who is likely to assist, or any other adult likely to assist.

g. DISPOSITION OF CASES

Because of the principles contained in the Young Offenders Act, the tendency is to look to the rehabilitation of the young person, and not to punishment. This means that vast numbers of cases never reach court.

Alternative measures are often used instead of judicial proceedings. This may involve some form of probation supervision. These alternative measures will require the young person to accept responsibility for the offence, and accordingly the youth must first be advised of the right to be represented by counsel and be given a reasonable opportunity to consult with counsel.

Where a case proceeds to court, and there is a finding of guilt, there is a range of dispositions available to the court. It has the power to commit a young person to custody for a period of up to two years, or three years for the most serious offences (those carrying a maximum penalty of life imprisonment in adult court).

The court can also order that the young person be detained for treatment. It can impose a fine of up to $1 000, make compensation orders, community service orders, and so on. It can also give an absolute discharge with no form of penalty. There can also be probation for up to two years. However, a detention is viewed as a last resort form of disposition. The court will always avoid this except in the most aggravated cases. The judge has broad powers to order medical reports or probation reports to assist in finding an appropriate disposition.

h. TRIALS IN YOUTH COURT

Trials in youth court follow the same rules as trials in adult court (see chapters 26 and 27). One exception is that the proceedings for summary conviction offences apply, and therefore there are no preliminary hearings in youth court even for serious indictable offences.

Statements made by a youth to a police officer can be used as evidence provided —

(a) the statement was made voluntarily,

(b) the youth knew he or she was under no obligation to give a statement at the time it was made,

(c) the youth knew the statement might be used as evidence, and

(d) the youth was given the right to have legal counsel or a parent or other adult person present.

These rules do not apply in the cases of spontaneous oral statements to a police officer before there has been an opportunity to advise the young person of legal rights.

i. TRANSFER TO ORDINARY COURT

A young person who is 14 years of age and charged with an indictable offence (except minor ones such as theft under $1 000), may be transferred to adult court. This can only be done where the youth court decides, after hearing evidence, that the interests of society and the needs of the young person require transfer to adult court.

In deciding whether to transfer to adult court, the youth court must consider the following things:

(a) The seriousness of the alleged offence

(b) The age, maturity, character, and background of the young person and any prior court record

(c) Adequacy of the Young Offenders Act to deal with the circumstances of the case

(d) Availability of treatment or correctional resources at the youth court level

(e) Representations made to the court by the young person or the attorney general

(f) Any other factors the court considers relevant

Where the court makes an order to transfer or deny transfer, it must state reasons for its decision.

j. PROTECTION OF PRIVACY OF YOUNG PERSONS

The identity of a young offender must not be published in connection with the offence alleged, or a report of the hearing, adjudication, disposition, or appeal concerning the matter. It is also forbidden to publish any information that may serve to identify the young person. A violation of this provision is an indictable offence carrying imprisonment for up to two years, or a summary conviction offence.

In addition, where the court believes that information being presented to the court would be seriously injurious or prejudicial to the young person being dealt with, or to a young person or child who is a witness in the proceedings, or a young person or a child who is a victim of the offence charged, or that it would be in the interest of public morals, public order, or the administration of justice to exclude the public from the courtroom, the judge may make an order for exclusion.

33
ELECTRONIC SURVEILLANCE BY POLICE

The Protection of Privacy Act legalizes wiretapping by police in this country.

The act provides legal means for law enforcement authorities to intercept and record telephone conversations and any other kind of oral or telecommunication. Surreptitious interception of private communications through wiretapping and other devices has always been carried on by the RCMP and other police agencies in Canada. However, in the past it was regarded as an invasion of privacy, perhaps an illegal trespass, and was thought to be unlawful (and in fact, from 1960, may have been illegal under the Bill of Rights).

This situation usually led police to deny that wiretapping existed, except in rare cases where they sought to introduce the tape-recording as evidence. Most of the time the information obtained by electronic surveillance was used to make further investigations.

Wiretapping has traditionally been used most often against persons involved in alleged organized crime and against persons alleged to be political dissenters.

Evidence obtained from wiretapping is now being used in many more cases. It is probably much more common in Canada on a per capita basis than it is in the United States.

a. WHAT TYPES OF COMMUNICATIONS CAN BE LEGALLY INTERCEPTED?

If police have an authorization from a judge, they can intercept any type of private conversation. This can include phone calls, conversation in meetings in private offices, conversations in interview rooms in the police stations, in public buildings or even in courthouses or jails. Hyperbolic microphones could be used to intercept conversations from a long distance.

b. PROCEDURES TO BE FOLLOWED FOR LEGAL WIRETAPS

Police must first obtain an authorization from a superior court judge. In order to do this there must be an application to a judge of a superior court or a judge of a county or district court signed by the attorney general of the province or the Solicitor General of Canada.

The application must be supported by an affidavit of a police officer or a prosecutor. The affidavit must state: the particulars of the offence being investigated; the facts which justify the belief that an authorization should be given; the type of private communication intended to be intercepted; the names, addresses, and occupations, if known, of all persons whose communications police believe may assist the investigation of the offence; a general description of the nature and location of the place where the private communications are to be intercepted; and the manner of interception to be used.

It must also state the period for which the authorization is required, which is a maximum of 60 days. The police officer must swear in the affidavit that other investigative procedures have been tried and have failed, or why they are unlikely to succeed, or that the urgency of the matter is so great that it would be impractical to investigate using ordinary methods.

The judge will grant an authorization if he or she is satisfied that it is in the best interests of justice and that other investigative procedures have been tried and have failed, or are unlikely to succeed, or that the matter has such great urgency that it would be impractical to investigate by other means.

An authorization will allow police to wiretap and record telephone conversations, or use other methods of electronic surveillance, employing electromagnetic acoustic, mechanical, or other devices.

After the initial period of the authorization, it can be renewed for a further period of up to 60 days. Documents used to obtain the authorization are secret and must be placed by the judge in a sealed packet.

c. WHAT OFFENCES CAN BE INVESTIGATED BY WIRETAPPING?

Legal wiretapping is available for a wide range of indictable offences, but not for investigation of summary offences, such as common assault or causing a disturbance. Nor is it available for driving offences, such as impaired driving, hit and run, or driving under suspension.

Some of the offences for which electronic surveillance may be authorized are —

- treason,
- forgery,
- hijacking
- possession of explosives or prohibited weapons,
- bribery,
- perjury,
- rape,
- unlawful interception of telecommunication,
- murder,
- kidnapping,
- extortion,
- breaking and entering,
- possession of property obtained by crime,
- theft from mail,
- fraud,
- manipulation of stock exchange transactions,
- arson,
- keeping a gaming or betting house,
- assault causing bodily harm,

- theft over $200,
- trafficking, importing, or exporting a narcotic under the Food and Drugs Act,
- smuggling narcotics or liquor or other contraband under the Customs Act,
- unlawful distillation or selling of spirits under the Excise Act,

or any other offence under the Criminal Code carrying a sentence of five years or more that there are reasonable and probable grounds to believe is part of a pattern of criminal activity planned by a number of persons acting in concert.

d. CONVERSATIONS WITH UNDERCOVER AGENTS OR INFORMERS

There are some important exceptions to the wiretapping laws. For example, no legal authorization is required to record a conversation between two parties where one of the parties to the conversation consents to it being recorded. This would cover the situation of an undercover officer in dealing with a target suspect. The undercover officer who is one of the people involved in the conversation, either as an originator of it or as a receiver of it, can consent to the interception or recording of the conversation.

In many cases, the officer will indicate consent by carrying a body-pack (hidden microphone or tape-recorder) for the sole purpose of recording the conversation. In such cases, the conversation is admissible against the suspect in court, even though it was obtained without lawful authorization. As well, the police officer involved in the interception would be immune to prosecution under the wiretap provisions.

Obviously the same kind of principles apply where the suspect has a conversation with a person who is a police informer. The informer can consent to the recording of the conversation by police, or personally record the conversation by means of body-pack tape-recorder or microphone and the target person has no recourse against this.

In addition, if it is intended later to use the conversation as evidence in court, the informer can appear as a witness and give testimony as to his or her consent to the interception of the conversation.

There is some suggestion in the court decisions that an associate of an accused person who later becomes a police witness can give an *ex post facto* (after the fact) consent to the wiretap.

That is, the informer witness can actually consent to the conversation being intercepted many months after the actual interception even though he or she did not know that the conversation was being recorded at the time, and can do so on the basis of making a deal to have the charge dropped against himself or herself. The courts have ruled that a consent obtained in this manner might be acceptable under the law.

e. HOW LONG DOES A WIRETAP CONTINUE?

The maximum period for which a wiretap may continue is 60 days, although it may be for any lesser time. There can be a renewal for a further 60 days and there can be any number of renewals as long as the investigation is continuing.

f. DOES A SUSPECT HAVE THE RIGHT TO KNOW IF HIS OR HER PHONE HAS BEEN WIRETAPPED?

The provincial attorney general or the Solicitor General of Canada is required to notify persons whom they have wiretapped. However, there is provision in the Criminal Code for extending the period for giving this notice up to three years. Under the original form of the wiretap law, the suspect was entitled to notice 90 days after the wiretap was removed. This was amended by putting in the three-year period.

At the end of each year, the Solicitor General of Canada must prepare a report of all wiretap authorizations.

In addition, the attorney general of each province must at the end of each year prepare and publish a report relating to all authorizations and the interceptions made.

g. DOES A PERSON HAVE ANY RIGHT TO PREVENT WIRETAPS?

There is nothing in the statute that forbids you from taking steps to find out if your phone is wiretapped. In fact, there are private firms that will do a sweep of premises to determine whether any wiretaps or microphones are in place. You are entitled to take steps to preserve your right to privacy and to prevent interception of your private conversations.

h. WHAT ARE THE PENALTIES FOR ILLEGAL WIRETAPPING?

A police officer (or anyone else) who intercepts a private communication illegally can be prosecuted under the Criminal Code. The maximum penalty for an illegal interception of private communications is five years in jail; for illegally using or disclosing the private communication or a part of it, or the fact of its existence, the maximum penalty is two years.

Where a person is convicted of one of these offences, the victim of the illegal wiretap is entitled to apply for an order that the felon pay up to $5 000 in damages. In addition, the possession, sale, or purchase of any electromagnetic acoustic or mechanical device that is primarily used for unauthorized interception of private communications is an indictable offence, carrying a maximum penalty of up to two years.

i. WHAT USE CAN BE MADE OF EVIDENCE OBTAINED THROUGH WIRETAPS?

The law allows prosecutors to use tape-recordings of private conversations as evidence in criminal trials. In fact, as noted above, wiretap evidence is becoming increasingly common. It has been a favored form of evidence used in conspiracy prosecutions where it is necessary to show agreement or a meeting of the minds of the co-accused.

In order to use the evidence, a notice of the intention to use it along with a transcript of the alleged conversations must be given to the accused person at a reasonable time prior to the trial.

Wiretap conversations cannot be used as evidence unless they have been legally obtained. However, the law also provides that the judge may overlook a defect or irregularity in procedure in deciding whether the transcript of the wiretapped conversation is admissible in evidence. It remains to be seen as to how widely or how narrowly judges will construe this legal loophole.

In addition, even where the wiretapped evidence is not admissible, evidence obtained directly or indirectly as a result of the information in the intercepted communication, so-called "derivative evidence," may still be admissible.

A judge can reject the evidence where he or she takes the view that the admission of it would bring the administration of justice into disrepute.

The test of whether the administration of justice has been brought into disrepute by illegally obtained evidence is obviously a determination that leaves a lot of discretion to the trial judge. Again, the law is not yet clear as to the boundaries of the rules that the judges will apply.

j. CONVERSATIONS WITH LAWYERS

No wiretaps can be authorized to intercept communications at the office or residence of a lawyer or any other place ordinarily used by a lawyer for the purpose of consulting with clients, unless a judge is satisfied that there are reasonable grounds to believe that the lawyer or anyone else in the law office is about to become a party to an offence.

Where a judge is satisfied that there are reasonable grounds to believe that the lawyer is about to become a party to a criminal offence, the judge is permitted to grant the authorization, but must include in it terms and conditions to protect privileged communications between the lawyers and their clients.

34
REMEDIES

a. WHAT CAN YOU DO?

We have mentioned the possibility of bringing action against the police for illegal actions. Police misconduct can be remedied by suing the offending officer for damages in a civil court, by laying a criminal charge, or both.

In these proceedings, you should have witnesses. Otherwise, the court hearing the allegations against the police officer will have to choose between your word and the word of the officer. In cases where there is an independent witness, the court may be persuaded by the evidence of the witness.

There is a range of new remedies available against abuse of authority under the Charter of Rights and Freedoms. These remedies may include a court ruling that evidence obtained illegally cannot be used in the trial of a charge against you; the quashing of charges or staying of proceedings brought against you; or dismissal of the charge on the basis of an infringement or denial of constitutional rights. Remedies may also include an award of damages or court costs. The potential range of remedies is examined in the following sections.

b. CIVIL ACTIONS FOR ABUSE OF AUTHORITY

Civil actions may include law suits for damages for battery, false arrest or imprisonment, or malicious prosecution.

In civil court an action for damages is commenced by issuing a writ. The suing party, called the plaintiff, will normally retain legal counsel to prosecute such an action.

An *assault* is any touching of your person without your consent. An assault may arise as a threat. For example, suppose a police officer says he or she is going to use force if you do not consent to the arrest. This may be an assault against you even though you do not actually resist the arrest. Your co-operation on the basis that you believe you will be assaulted if you do not co-operate does not amount to a consent to the otherwise illegal arrest.

Another example could arise where a police officer requests that you come to the stationhouse but does not actually arrest you. You ask what the charge is and whether you are under arrest and the officer says that you are not going to be charged but are being taken for further investigations. This is an unlawful arrest. You are entitled to object and to resist. If you are forcibly taken to the station, it amounts to an assault, possibly a battery (if you are struck), a false arrest, and a false imprisonment.

False imprisonment is complete deprivation of liberty for any time, however short, without lawful cause. The restraint may result from actual physical force amounting to an assault or from fear that force will be used. Anyone who helps to continue the wrongful detention is party to it.

For example, in one successful suit, a twenty-year-old youth sued two police officers for assault and false imprisonment. Shortly after midnight the plaintiff and a friend were walking toward the friend's home.

Two plainclothes officers in a marked police car stopped them. One officer asked for identification, but the plaintiff refused and asked the officer to identify himself first. The officer produced a badge, but wouldn't give his name. The plaintiff again refused to identify himself. A scuffle ensued and the plaintiff was injured. The officers forced him into the police car and took him to the station. He was not given any reason for the arrest.

Police testified that they stopped the two young men because they were sauntering along the street and because of their attire, which the court found was not particularly distinctive. There had been break-ins in the neighborhood a few nights before, and it was reported that a person wearing rubber-soled shoes was involved. The plaintiff's companion was wearing rubber-soled shoes.

The court found that the police had no reasonable and probable grounds to believe the plaintiff had committed or was about to commit an indictable offence and there were no vagrancy circumstances. They could ask, but not compel him to identify himself. He was entitled to know whether he was under arrest and on what charge. He did not have to submit to imprisonment unless he knew the reason for it. He was entitled to resist. The plaintiff recovered damages and court costs.

A defence of justification is available to a police officer under Section 25 of the Criminal Code if he makes an error, such as arresting the wrong person, provided he has acted "on reasonable and probable grounds" and has not used more force than is necessary to make the arrest. The question is what amounts to reasonable and probable grounds in a given case.

An officer cannot make an arrest based on mere suspicion. There must be rational reasons for the actions. There must be some basis for believing that the arrest is justified at the time it is made, based on the real facts of the situation and the evidence available.

If someone maliciously charges you with an offence and there is no evidence to support the charge, you may have an action for damages for *malicious prosecution*. Malice can be proved by showing that the real intention was to injure you rather than to seek justice. You can sue the person who started the proceedings against you and anyone else who had a part in your being prosecuted.

c. CRIMINAL CHARGES FOR ABUSE OF AUTHORITY

Criminal charges may be laid against police officers who have employed unlawful arrest or search procedures. Any person has a right to lay a criminal charge against a police officer who commits an offence. The first step is to go before a justice of the peace in order to swear an information alleging the offence. It is necessary to identify the particular officer by name or description (such as badge number, height, weight, hair color, etc.). Normally the police department is co-operative in assisting in identification of the officers involved.

The justice of the peace may interview the complainant. He or she may consult with the prosecutor before deciding whether to accept the charge. The complainant, however, has the right to lay the charge.

Some of the charges that might be appropriate in situations of police misconduct are the following.

(a) A charge of common assault can be laid against an officer who has made an illegal arrest or search of a person without his or her consent.

(b) A charge of breaking and entering can be laid against police officers who break into a dwelling-house without a warrant.

(c) Theft charges may be laid against police officers who take anything without lawful authority.

(d) Mischief charges can also be laid where there is damage to doors or windows.

d. THE EFFECT OF THE CHARTER OF RIGHTS AND FREEDOMS

Section 24(1) of the Charter of Rights and Freedoms, dealing with enforcement of rights, provides as follows:

> 24.(1) Anyone whose rights or freedoms, as guaranteed by this Charter, have been infringed or denied may apply to a court of competent jurisdiction to obtain such remedy as the court considers appropriate and just in the circumstances.

In relation to police, prosecutors, and courts, the fundamental rights that we are concerned with have been dealt with in preceding chapters.

There are, of course, several other rights, including the right against being subjected to cruel and unusual treatment or punishment, the right against having self-incriminating evidence used in subsequent proceedings, the right to an interpreter, and the right to use English or French in any of the higher courts.

There are also the fundamental freedoms, including freedom of conscience and religion, freedom of thought, belief, opinion, and expression (including freedom of the press and other media of communication), freedom of peaceful assembly, and freedom of association.

There are also specific rules for criminal proceedings, such as the rule against double jeopardy. This means if a person has been acquitted of an offence, he or she is entitled not to be tried for it again; or if found guilty and punished, not to be tried or punished for it again.

There is also the right to equality before and under the law and the right to equal protection and benefit of the law. Other rights are beyond the scope of this particular book.

The effect of Section 24(1) is that where any of these rights or freedoms have been infringed or denied by any police officer, prosecutor, court, or other agent of the federal or provincial government, the person whose rights have been so infringed or denied is entitled to apply to a court of competent jurisdiction to obtain "such remedy as the court considers appropriate and just in the circumstances."

e. REMEDIES AVAILABLE UNDER SECTION 24(1)

In Canada, provincial courts or magistrates are appointed by each provincial government. As mentioned earlier, these courts deal with many criminal cases. There is no doubt that these are courts of competent jurisdiction for the purpose of enforcing the Charter rights when they are holding a trial of a criminal case.

In addition, there are two sets of courts with federally appointed judges: the federal court and those which are administered by the provincial governments, such as the supreme court or high court of the province, and the court of appeal of the province.

Provincially administered courts also deal with criminal cases. Again, there is no doubt that these courts are courts of competent criminal jurisdiction. They also have jurisdiction to entertain civil actions for declarations of rights, or for damages for assault and battery, false arrest, false imprisonment, malicious prosecution, and so on.

The federal court of Canada deals with lawsuits involving the federal government on matters that are exclusively within the jurisdiction of the federal government. It does not deal with criminal trials but is also a court of competent jurisdiction to apply the Charter of Rights to matters falling within its authority.

The question of which court can provide which remedy under the Charter has not been finally determined and there is no definition of what remedies are available under the Charter. The Charter simply says that competent courts can provide appropriate and just remedies where there has been a breach of a person's rights under the Charter. What are appropriate and just remedies? At the moment there is no answer to this. The constitution is not specific and there are numerous possibilities. Here are some of those possibilities.

1. Motion to quash charges

When the principles of fundamental justice under Section 7 of the Charter have been breached, or there has been an unreasonable delay in informing an accused person of the specific offence, a judge may grant a motion to quash the charges, thereby effectively ending the prosecution.

The Supreme Court of Canada has held that where the trial has not proceeded within a reasonable time, the minimum remedy available is a stay of proceedings to stop the charges.

2. Dismissal of charges

Where a court finds a violation of the right to be dealt with in accordance with the principles of fundamental justice, or arbitrary detention or imprisonment, or a denial of the right to counsel, or unreasonable delay informing the accused of a specific offence, or not trying the person within a reasonable time, the judge could dismiss the charge on the basis of such denials of Charter rights.

3. Remedies in sentencing

A court could fashion remedies by an appropriate sentence where the accused's rights under the Charter have been violated. For example, although a judge may find the accused guilty, he or she may consider that the right to counsel was violated and use that as a ground for granting a conditional or absolute discharge, so that the finding of guilt does not result in a conviction. Or the judge could provide a suspended sentence and probation or a fine, rather than a jail term.

Courts have a fair amount of latitude in sentencing matters and this would be an expedient method of remedying violations of Charter rights.

4. Other remedies

Other remedies could include an award of damages or court costs or counsel fees.

Remedies could also be sought in courts other than the trial court, such as the superior court of the province. These remedies could be damages for wrongful arrest, false imprisonment or malicious prosecution, or damages for the violation of a Charter right. That is, the Constitution may create new personal injury actions which would be in the nature of damages for violation of constitutional rights. This would be a novel development in Canadian law. It remains to be seen whether the courts will interpret the Charter in this way.

Other remedies could include such things as granting a writ of replevin to an accused thereby ordering the return of a sample of blood that has been illegally obtained. There have been some lower court decisions where this has been done after a blood sample was illegally taken in a drinking-driving investigation.

It will be clear from the foregoing that there is a large range of remedies that a court might consider appropriate and just within the meaning of Section 24(1). There is no way to predict precisely how this section will be interpreted by the courts. There is room for a great deal of legal ingenuity in this area. One thing is certain, Canadians are a lot better off with the Charter than they were before when they had virtually no remedy for violations of civil rights.

f. REMEDIES AVAILABLE UNDER SECTION 24(2)

Canada has moved a long distance away from the doctrine that illegally obtained evidence is admissible. In the new Charter of Rights and Freedoms, Section 24(2) provides:

> Where, in proceedings under subsection (1) a court concludes that evidence was obtained in a manner that infringed or denied any rights or freedoms guaranteed by this Charter, the evidence shall be excluded if it is established that, having regard to all the circumstances, the admission of it in the proceedings would bring the administration of justice into disrepute.

This does not mean that every time evidence is obtained in a manner that infringes or denies a Charter right or freedom that it will be excluded. Nor does it mean that all evidence obtained by denial or infringement of Charter rights will be excluded.

However, where the accused is able to establish to the satisfaction of the judge that the admission of the evidence into the trial "would bring the administration of justice into disrepute," the evidence will be rejected.

Section 24(2) may have application in the following kinds of situations.

Where a search has been conducted without a warrant and the defence is able to show that there were no reasonable grounds to conduct the search, the trial judge may reject the evidence on the basis that it was obtained by an unreasonable search or seizure. Further, where a search warrant was obtained, but is found by the trial judge to be wanting either because of a lack of information supplied to obtain it, or because of the way that the initial information was obtained, again the evidence may be rejected on the basis that it was obtained as a result of an unreasonable search.

Where a suspect has been arbitrarily detained or imprisoned, contrary to constitutional rights under Section 9 (the right not to be arbitrarily detained or imprisoned) and a confession is extracted, a court could reject the evidence of the confession.

Further, assuming the confession is inadmissible, suppose, as a result of the confession, police find a gun or knife used to commit an offence. Should this secondary or derivative evidence be admissible or inadmissible in court? Here again is a threshold issue that the courts will be called upon to resolve.

A related issue arises where the police obtain a confession without advising the suspect of his or her right to retain and instruct counsel without delay. The Supreme Court of Canada has held that such a violation leads the court to reject the confession as having been improperly obtained.

Many other issues must be resolved in considering this section. For example, what sorts of infringements or denials of Charter rights bring the administration of justice into disrepute? Does any denial of the right to counsel or the failure of police to advise a suspect of his or her constitutional right to consult a lawyer bring the administration of justice into disrepute? Does every form of arbitrary detention and every unreasonable search bring the administration of justice into disrepute? If not, in what circumstances is the administration of justice brought into disrepute?

The Supreme Court of Canada has made some initial rulings on virtually all of these issues. However, it remains to be seen what the full implications of these decisions will be. So far the decisions amount to, in essence, guidelines which lower courts are struggling to apply on a daily basis.

APPENDIX

CONSTITUTION ACT, 1982
PART I

Canadian Charter of Rights and Freedoms

Whereas Canada is found upon principles that recognize the supremacy of God and the rule of law:

1. The *Canadian Charter of Rights and Freedoms* guarantees the rights and freedoms set out in it subject only to such reasonable limits prescribed by law as can be demonstrably justified in a free and democratic society.

2. Everyone has the following fundamental freedoms:

(a) freedom of conscience and religion;

(b) freedom of thought, belief, opinion and expression, including freedom of the press and other media of communication;

(c) freedom of peaceful assembly; and

(d) freedom of association.

3. Every citizen of Canada has the right to vote in an election of members of the House of Commons or of a legislative assembly and to be qualified for membership therein.

4. (1) No House of Commons and no legislative assembly shall continue for longer than five years from the date fixed for the return of the writs at a general election of its members.

(2) In time of real or apprehended war, invasion or insurrection, a House of Commons may be continued by Parliament and a legislative assembly may be continued by the legislature beyond five years if such continuation is not opposed by the votes of more than one-third of the members of the House of Commons or the legislative assembly, as the case may be.

5. There shall be a sitting of Parliament and of each legislature at least once every twelve months.

6. (1) Every citizen of Canada has the right to enter, remain in and leave Canada.

(2) Every citizen of Canada and every person who has the status of a permanent resident of Canada has the right

(a) to move to and take up residence in any province; and

(b) to pursue the gaining of a likelihood in any province.

(3) The rights specified in subsection (2) are subject to

(a) any laws or practices of general application in force in a province other than those that discriminate among persons primarily on the basis of province of present or previous residence; and

(b) any laws providing for reasonable residency requirements as a qualification for the receipt of publicly provided social services.

(4) Subsections (2) and (3) do not preclude any law, program or activity that has as its object the amelioration in a province of conditions of individuals in that province who are socially or economically disadvantaged if the rate of employment in that province is below the rate of employment in Canada.

7. Everyone has the right to life, liberty and security of the person and the right not to be deprived thereof except in accordance with the principles of fundamental justice.

8. Everyone has the right to be secure against unreasonable search or seizure.

9. Everyone has the right not to be arbitrarily detained or imprisoned.

10. Everyone has the right on arrest or detention

(a) to be informed promptly of the reasons therefor;

(b) to retain and instruct counsel without delay and to be informed of that right; and

(c) to have the validity of the detention determined by way of *habeas corpus* and to be released if the detention is not lawful.

11. Any person charged with an offence has the right

(a) to be informed without unreasonable delay of the specific offence;

(b) to be tried within a reasonable time;

(c) not to be compelled to be a witness in proceedings against that person in respect of the offence;

(d) to be presumed innocent until proven guilty according to law in a fair and public hearing by an independent and impartial tribunal;

(e) not to be denied reasonable bail without just cause;

(f) except in the case of an offence under military law tried before a military tribunal, to the benefit of trial by jury where the maximum punishment for the offence is imprisonment for five years or a more severe punishment;

(g) not to be found guilty on account of any act or omission unless, at the time of the act or omission, it constituted an offence under Canadian or international law or was criminal according to the general principles of law recognized by the community of nations;

(h) if finally acquitted of the offence, not to be tried for it again and, if finally found guilty and punished for the offence, not to be tried or punished for it again; and

(i) if found guilty of the offence and if the punishment for the offence has been varied between the time of commission and the time of sentencing, to the benefit of the lesser punishment.

12. Everyone has the right not to be subjected to any cruel and unusual treatment or punishment.

13. A witness who testifies in any proceedings has the right not to have any incriminating evidence so given used to incriminate that witness in any other proceedings, except in a prosecution for perjury or for the giving of contradictory evidence.

14. A party of witness in any proceedings who does not understand or speak the language in which the proceedings are conducted or who is deaf has the right to the assistance of an interpreter.

15. (1) Every individual is equal before and under the law and has the right to the equal protection and equal benefit of the law without discrimination and, in particular, without discrimination based on race, national or ethnic origin, colour, religion, sex, age or mental or physical disability.

(2) Subsection (1) does not preclude any law, program or activity that has as its object the amelioration of conditions of disadvantaged individuals or groups including those that are disadvantaged because of race, national or ethnic origin, colour, religion, sex, age or mental or physical disability.

16. (1) English and French are the official languages of Canada and have equality of status and equal rights and privileges as to their use in all institutions of the Parliament and government of Canada.

(2) English and French are the official languages of New Brunswick and have equality of status and equal rights and privileges as to their use in all institutions of the legislature and government of New Brunswick.

(3) Nothing in this Charter limits the authority of Parliament or a legislature to advance the equality of status or use of English and French.

17. (1) Everyone has the right to use English or French in any debates and other proceedings of Parliament.

(2) Everyone has the right to use English or French in any debates and other proceedings of the legislature of New Brunswick.

18. (1) The statutes, records and journals of Parliament shall be printed and published in English and French and both language versions are equally authoritative.

(2) The statutes, records and journals of the legislature of New Brunswick shall be printed and published in English and French and both language versions are equally authoritative.

19. (1) Either English or French may be used by any person in, or in any pleading in or process issuing from, any court established by Parliament.

(2) Either English or French may be used by any person in, or in any pleading in or process issuing from, any court of New Brunswick.

20. (1) Any member of the public in Canada has the right to communicate with, and to receive available services from any head or central office of an institution of the Parliament or government of Canada in English or French, and has the same right with respect to any other office of any such institution where

(a) there is a significant demand for communications with and services from that office in such language; or

(b) due to the nature of the office, it is reasonable that communications with and services from that office be available in both English and French.

(2) Any member of the public in New Brunswick has the right to communicate with, and to receive available services from, any office of an institution of the legislature or government of New Brunswick in English or French.

21. Nothing in Sections 16 to 20 abrogates or derogates from any right, privilege or obligation with respect to the English and French languages, or either of them, that exists or is continued by virtue of any other provision of the Constitution of Canada.

22. Nothing is Sections 16 to 20 abrogates or derogates from any legal or customary right or privilege acquired or enjoyed either before or after the coming into force of this Charter with respect to any language that is not English or French.

23. (1) Citizens of Canada

(a) whose first language learned and still understood is that of the English or French linguistic minority population of the province in which they reside, or

(b) who have received their primary school instruction in Canada in English or French and reside in a province where the language in which they received that instruction is the language of the English or French linguistic minority population of the

of the English or French linguistic minority population of the province,
have the right to have their children receive primary and secondary school instruction in that language in that province.

(2) Citizens of Canada of whom any child has received or is receiving primary or secondary school instruction in English or French in Canada, have the right to have all their children receive primary and secondary school instruction in the same language.

(3) The right of citizens of Canada under subsections (1) and (2) to have their children receive primary and secondary school instruction in the language of the English or French linguistic minority population of a province

(a) applies wherever in the province the number of children of citizens who have such a right is sufficient to warrant the provision to them out of public funds of minority language instruction; and

(b) includes, where the number of those children so warrants, the right to have them receive that instruction in minority language educational facilities provided out of public funds.

24. (1) Anyone whose rights or freedoms, as guaranteed by this Charter, have been infringed or denied may apply to a court of competent jurisdiction to obtain such remedy as the court considers appropriate and just in the circumstances.

(2) Where, in proceedings under subsection (1), a court concludes that evidence was obtained in a manner that infringed or denied any rights or freedoms guaranteed by this Charter, the evidence shall be excluded if it is established that, having regard to all the circumstances, the admission of it in the proceedings would bring the administration of justice into disrepute.

25. The guarantee in this Charter of certain rights and freedoms shall not be construed so as to abrogate or derogate from any aboriginal, treaty or other rights or freedoms that pertain to the aboriginal peoples of Canada including

(a) any rights or freedoms that have been recognized by the Royal Proclamation of October 7, 1763; and

(b) any rights or freedoms that may be acquired by the aboriginal peoples of Canada by way of land claims settlement.

26. The guarantee in this Charter of certain rights and freedoms shall not be construed as denying the existence of any other rights or freedoms that exist in Canada.

27. This Charter shall be interpreted in a manner consistent with the preservation and enhancement of the multicultural heritage of Canadians.

28. Notwithstanding anything in this Charter, the rights and freedoms referred to in it are guaranteed equally to male and female persons.

29. Nothing in this Charter abrogates or derogates from any rights or privileges guaranteed by or under the Constitution of Canada in respect of denominational, separate or dissentient schools.

30. A reference in this Charter to a province or to the legislative assembly or legislature of a province shall be deemed to include a reference to the Yukon Territory and the Northwest Territories, or to the appropriate legislative authority thereof, as the case may be.

31. Nothing in this Charter extends the legislative powers of any body or authority.

32. (1) This Charter applies

(a) to the parliament and government of Canada in respect of all matters within the authority of Parliament including all matters relating to the Yukon Territory and Northwest Territories; and

(b) to the legislature and government of each province in respect of all matters within the authority of the legislature of each province.

(2) Notwithstanding subsection (1), Section 15 shall not have effect until three years after this section comes into force.

33. (1) Parliament or the legislature of a province may expressly declare in an Act of Parliament or of the legislature, as the case may be, that the act or a provision thereof shall operate notwithstanding a provision included in Section 2 or Sections 7 to 15 of this Charter.

(2) An act or a provision of an act in respect of which a declaration made under this section is in effect shall have such operation as it would have but for the provision of this Charter referred to in the declaration.

(3) A declaration made under subsection (1) shall cease to have effect five years after it comes into force or on such earlier date as may be specified in the declaration.

(4) Parliament or a legislature of a province may re-enact a declaration made under subsection (1).

(5) Subsection (3) applies in respect of a re-enactment made under subsection (4).

PART VII
GENERAL

52. (1) The Constitution of Canada is the supreme law of Canada, and any law that is inconsistent with the provisions of the Constitution is, to the extent of the inconsistency, of no force or effect.

(2) The Constitution of Canada includes

(a) the Canada Act, 1982, including this Act;

(b) the Acts and orders referred to in the schedule; and

(c) any amendment to any act or order referred to in paragraph (a) or (b).

(3) Amendments to the Constitution of Canada shall be made only in accordance with the authority contained in the Constitution of Canada.

53. (1) The enactments referred to in Column 1 of the schedule are hereby repealed or amended to the extent indicated in Column II thereof and, unless repealed, shall continue as law in Canada under the names set out in Column III thereof.

(2) Every enactment, except the Canada Act, 1982, that refers to an enactment referred to in the schedule by the name in Column I thereof is hereby amended by substituting for that name the corresponding name in Column III thereof, and any British North America Act not referred to in the schedule may be cited as the Constitution Act followed by the year and number, if any, of its enactment.

CANADIAN ORDER FORM
SELF-COUNSEL SERIES

01/89

NATIONAL TITLES

___	Abbreviations & Acronyms	5.95
___	Asking Questions	7.95
___	Assertiveness for Managers	9.95
___	Basic Accounting	6.95
___	Be a Better Manager	8.95
___	Better Book for Getting Hired	9.95
___	Between the Sexes	8.95
___	Business Etiquette Today	7.95
___	Business Guide to Effective Speaking	6.95
___	Business Guide to Profitable Customer Relations	7.95
___	Business Writing Workbook	9.95
___	Buying and Selling a Small Business	7.95
___	Civil Rights	8.95
___	Collection Techniques for the Small Business	4.95
___	Complete Guide to Home Contracting	19.95
___	Conquering Compulsive Eating	5.95
___	Credit, Debt, and Bankruptcy	7.95
___	Criminal Procedure in Canada	16.95
___	Death in the Family	8.95
___	Design Your Own Logo	9.95
___	Editing Your Newsletter	14.95
___	Entrepreneur's Self-Assessment Guide	9.95
___	Environmental Law	8.95
___	Every Retailer's Guide to Loss Prevention	
___	Family Ties That Bind	7.95
___	Federal Incorporation and Business Guide	14.95
___	Financial Control for the Small Business	6.95
___	Financial Freedom on $5 a Day	7.95
___	Fit After Fifty	
___	For Sale By Owner	6.95
___	Forming and Managing a Non-Profit Organization in Canada	12.95
___	Franchising in Canada	6.95
___	Fundraising	5.50
___	Getting Elected	8.95
___	Getting Started	10.95
___	How to Advertise	7.95
___	How You Too Can Make a Million in the Mail Order Business	9.95
___	Immigrating to Canada	14.95
___	Immigrating to the U.S.A.	14.95
___	Keyboarding for Kids	7.95
___	Landlording in Canada	14.95
___	Learn to Type Fast	11.50
___	Managing Stress	7.95
___	Margo Oliver's Cookbook for Seniors	
___	Marketing Your Product	12.95
___	Marketing Your Service	12.95
___	Medical Law Handbook	6.95
___	Mike Grenby's Tax Tips	7.95
___	Teenagers and Suicide	
___	Mobile Retirement Handbook	9.95
___	Mortgages & Foreclosure	7.95
___	A Nanny For Your Child	7.95
___	Newcomer's Guide to the U.S.A.	12.95
___	Patent Your Own Invention	21.95
___	Planning for Financial Independence	11.95
___	Practical Guide to Financial Management	6.95
___	Practical Time Management	6.95
___	Radio Documentary Handbook	8.95
___	Ready-to-Use Business Forms	9.95
___	Retirement Guide for Canadians	9.95
___	Selling Strategies for Service Businesses	12.95
___	Small Business Guide to Employee Selection	6.95
___	Sport and Recreation Liability and You	
___	Start and Run a Profitable Beauty Salon	14.95
___	Start and Run a Profitable Consulting Business	12.95
___	Start and Run a Profitable Craft Business	10.95
___	Start and Run a Profitable Restaurant	10.95
___	Start and Run a Profitable Retail Business	11.95
___	Starting a Successful Business in Canada	12.95
___	Step-Parent Adoptions	12.95
___	Taking Care	7.95
___	Teenagers and Suicide	8.95
___	Travelwise	

	Upper Left-Hand Corner	10.95
	Wise and Healthy Living	
	Working Couples	5.50
	Write Right!	5.50

PROVINCIAL TITLES
Divorce Guide
❏ B.C. 9.95 ❏ Alberta 9.95 ❏ Saskatchewan 12.95
❏ Manitoba 11.95 ❏ Ontario 12.95
Employer/Employee Rights
❏ B.C. 7.95 ❏ Alberta 6.95 ❏ Ontario 6.95
Incorporation Guide
❏ B.C. 14.95 ❏ Alberta 14.95 ❏ Manitoba/Saskatchewan 12.95 ❏ Ontario 14.95
Landlord/Tenant Rights
❏ B.C. 7.95 ❏ Alberta 6.95 ❏ Ontario 7.95
Marriage & Family Law
❏ B.C. 7.95 ❏ Alberta 8.95 ❏ Ontario 7.95
Probate Guide
❏ B.C. 12.95 ❏ Alberta 10.95 ❏ Ontario 11.95
Real Estate Guide
❏ B.C. 8.95 ❏ Alberta 7.95 ❏ Ontario 8.50
Small Claims Court Guide
❏ B.C. 7.95 ❏ Alberta 7.50 ❏ Ontario 7.50
Wills
❏ B.C. 6.50 ❏ Alberta 6.50 ❏ Ontario 5.95
❏ Wills/Probate Procedure for Manitoba/Saskatchewan 5.95

PACKAGED FORMS
Divorce Forms
❏ B.C 11.95 ❏ Alberta 10.95 ❏ Saskatchewan 12.95
❏ Manitoba 10.95 ❏ Ontario 14.95
Incorporation
❏ B.C 14.95   ❏ Alberta 14.95 ❏ Saskatchewan 14.95
❏ Manitoba 14.95 ❏ Ontario 14.95 ❏ Federal 7.95
❏ Minute Books 17.95
❏ Power of Attorney Kit 9.95
Probate
❏ B.C. Administration 14.95 ❏ B.C. Probate 14.95
❏ Alberta 14.95 ❏ Ontario 15.50
❏ Rental Form Kit (B.C., Alberta, Saskatchewan, Ontario) 4.95
❏ Have You Made Your Will? 5.95
❏ If You Love Me Put It In Writing – Contract Kit 14.95
❏ If You Leave Me Put It In Writing – B.C. Separation Agreement Kit 14.95
Interim Agreement
❏ B.C. 2.50 ❏ Alberta 2.50 ❏ Ontario 2.50

Note: All prices subject to change without notice.
Books are available in book and department stores, or use the order form below. Please enclose cheque or money order (plus sales tax where applicable) or give us your MasterCard or Visa number (please include validation and expiry dates).

✂ ....

(PLEASE PRINT)
Name _____
Address _____
City _____ Province _____
Postal Code _____
❏ Visa/❏ MasterCard Number_____
Validation Date_____ Expiry Date _____
If order is under $20.00, add $1.00 for postage and handling.
Please send orders to:

SELF-COUNSEL PRESS
1481 Charlotte Road
North Vancouver, British Columbia   V7J 1H1
  ❏ Check here for free catalogue.